My Mother Can Beat Up Your Father

Danny Langdon

Son of Marian Orena Smith Langdon

PublISH AMERICA

PublishAmerica
Baltimore

First printing

ISBN: 1-4241-4023-4
PUBLISHED BY PUBLISHAMERICA, LLLP
www.publishamerica.com
Baltimore

Printed in the United States of America

Dedication

To our wonderful mother, who taught all her children by her example the meaning of being a caring and productive person in the world.

—Her Children

Acknowledgment

My Mother Can Beat Up Your Father speaks to the truth of the matter. I hope you understand that my claim that "my mother can beat up your father" was never meant to apply in the physical sense, but is rather a loving and humorous way to capture her overall character. She was a model of humanity. She embodied both man and woman at their very best. Her positive lessons provided a continuous legacy for her children.

I would like to thank my surviving sisters for their recollection of stories past. They had better memories than I when it came to certain events. Also, a special thanks to Michelle Hiskey Smith, one of our mother's 22 grandchildren who took the thoughtful step of recording for our history a conversation with her grandmother. Along with my own taped recording of an earlier conversation with my mother, these permanent histories serve not only as source material, but more importantly they capture that sweet and loving voice and character. Thank you as well to Mitchell Langdon Townley and his sister Kristen Townley Puckett for their wonderful poetic words. They reflect so well on the character and the love that her grandchildren, and 10 great-grandchildren had for her during her life. A special thanks to my wife for letting me live out the dreams, love, and aspirations my mother so longed for and wanted for each of her children. Thanks as well to our friend, Brenda Sample for reading and editing the final copy. My mother would have liked her very, very much, and they could have been such good friends. And thanks to my daughter, Johnilee, for her reading of the final stage of the manuscript. She confirmed for me that the story told was the one in my heart.

A special thanks to Jennifer Blaszka, and others of PublishAmerica, for making the book editing and production a joy.

Most of all, thanks to my mother for being Mother!

—Her son, Danny G.

Table of Contents

My Mother Can Beat Up Your Father

Few words could be more empowering to a boy than to proclaim, "My mother can beat up your father." In my case, this statement, used on occasion when necessary, was totally true. And every schoolyard bully, and other kid in town, knew it.

I always believed these few simple words about my mother. My mother could have taken on any man and have bested him in an argument or disputed point, if not in many cases, perhaps, physically. Fortunately, I am not aware that she ever had to prove her physical prowess in any situation with a man. But I did see her numerous times handle with finesse men in her business practice. It was natural, I guess, for some men to think they could get a better deal through a little bit of intimidation when negotiating to sell their scrap metal to her. But, they could not. She did, after all, operate on her own a successful scrap-metal business for 40 years in a small town nestled in southern Idaho. She had been widowed early in her life, and out of necessity taken on a business dominated by men. Indeed, she was one of the few women in business of any kind in the 1940s and for years thereafter. She knew the value of all things in her business and in life. She bought and sold scrap metal or "junk," as it was referred to in slang terms. Recycling was invented with the idea of collecting and selling scrap metal to support the war effort. She conducted her business fairly, and expected others to treat her fairly as well. And mostly they did.

Besides running her business on a full-time basis, our mother was a big part of the community of Twin Falls, Idaho—a respected citizen, leader of many community events, a model of service to others, a professional, working woman, provider of care to the needy, and most important to her and us—a loving mother to her eight children. She embodied through her deeds numerous lessons that we children learned and continue to live out today. These legacies from a wonderful mother are the lessons that all loving parents would want to pass on to their own children, but sometimes just don't quite know how to do. This book introduces you to an exceptional woman, and provides by numerous stories the lessons she taught us. Perhaps in your own way you can find similar experience for the positive lessons your own children will need to learn if they are to productive members of society. Mine is the memory of that fine woman—my mother—who could "beat up your father" and in the process be a wonderful example to her children and a role model to society.

It was really only as an adult that I learned and fully appreciated my mother's trials growing up. One has to wonder how she became the loving person she did, for at times those trials were daunting. Others might have folded under similar experiences in the turbulent period she grew up in from 1911 to 1928, and then as an adult in the Great Depression, Second World War and beyond. She had an inner strength, built on love from caring relatives and recognition of what little she had, so she could rise above these challenges to become a person with extraordinary values.

No, my mother would not really have beaten up your father, but on the other hand, she had a way about her that made you think she could—and would have if needed. I liked that about her. This is the story of an exceptional person who taught her children well by her example. Her story exemplifies the adage that we all learn from good examples.

The Beginning:
Childhood Abandonment
and Loving Care

Although our mother had a wonderful childhood by her own account, she never spoke much about it except to occasionally mention the things she cherished most. Her life, as we would come know of it, mostly started, from her frame of reference when she was 16 years of age. I will relate what we do know about her childhood before getting to what transpired at the age of 16 that set the tone for her adult life.

What we know of her childhood started with a not-so-uncommon tragedy that befalls many children today. Her parents divorced when she was but two years old. This event alone could have scarred her forever, but it didn't because of a caring grandmother. As if the divorce wasn't enough, she was seemingly abandoned forever by her mother, and left in the charge of a father who would drop in and out of her life. Having been abandoned by both parents in their own separate ways could have been devastating for any child, who could perhaps use it as an excuse to develop a negative view of life. But our mother survived the emotional and psychological pains. Our mother's fortitude and inner strength came not from those who walked or were pushed away from her, but rather from those who, while not members of her nuclear family, cared for and nurtured her despite the odds.

Born March 3, 1911 in Jamestown, New York, to Apollina Boehler and Hazel Jenner Smith, our mother was the first of two children, both girls, born 11 months apart. They named their first daughter, Marion Orena Smith, although later in life she renamed herself "Marian," as she preferred the more feminine spelling of her given name. Shortly after the birth of her sister Helen, their parents permanently parted. While the often-given explanation of why they separated seems simple enough, below the surface there lingered still unanswered questions to this day. Putting this story of our mother's life together has allowed me to develop what is perhaps a more accurate picture of why this separation occurred.

Mother's elders—principally her grandmother, aunt, and a couple of uncles—rarely talked about the girls' parents' divorce. They seemed to fear the truth, as if it would have somehow weakened the foundation of the family tree, even after everyone was grown and would have been no worse off for the full truth of the matter. When mentioned at all, a very short story was told: Apollina was said to have abandoned her husband and two infant daughters. She was supposed to have just left one day for no apparent reason. However, based on a conversation with Aunt Helen, our mother's sister, in later years, there is an alternative theory that seems more likely.

Apparently, Apollina had had an extramarital affair. Rather than face the scandal, the girls' father took the two children and quite literally forced his wife out of the house; she never returned. Given the attitude of people of that generation, this account seems quite plausible, although it is not the entire story. Thus, it appears that the two girls were literally snatched from their mother's arms and taken out of her life forever. Within a short time, they were sent off to live in a place almost as foreign as another country, and they never saw their mother again.

All we really know about Apollina was that she had a sister and two brothers. She was mostly of German stock, remarried a minister some time later, and remained in the city of Jamestown, New York, for all her life. Although our mother never saw her mother again, she did visit her mother's residence six months after her mother's death. On the occasion of her journey to her place of birth, our mother was being honored as Mother of the Year for the State of Idaho in 1952 and was traveling to New York City to celebrate nationally with other mothers so designated by their state of residence. During that trip, Mother visited Apollina's second husband, a Mr. Northrop. He and his mother took our mother out to dinner, and over a casual meal, she gained for the first time, after 41 years, some detailed insight into what her mother was like. From the conversation, she learned that they had many similarities in their overall loving character, service to others, and calmness of mind. The Northrops shared with her one of the few pictures Mother ever saw of her own mother, and gave her a prized black, bead necklace and a pair of matching earrings that had belonged to her. Imagine in only a couple of hours, learning more about your mother than you had in all the years leading up to that moment.

One can only imagine what might have passed between mother and daughter after so many years had they had the opportunity to actually meet. I am inclined to believe that their exchange would have been one, not about missed opportunity, but rather in shared similarities. Apollina was described by her second husband as a gentle, sweet person who was a good mother and served her own community, just as her daughter, our mother, did. It must have seemed tragic to him that the once "abandoned" child and now mature woman before him, now such an accomplished adult and community leader, had never really had the pleasure of knowing her own mother. At the same time, the loving wife and mother he knew so well had never witnessed the fine woman her daughter had become. An indiscretion had wrested two beautiful souls from each other. I believe they would have treasured one another; they would have healed a life-time ache. Instead, time, distance and finally death precluded such an experience. It is as sad as not being able to tell someone that you love them before it is too late.

The girls were four and three years of age when they were sent by their father from Jamestown, New York, to what was known as the Gimlet Siding, near the town of Hailey, Idaho. He had relatives there and sought to find some way to have the girls cared for as he seemed incapable of doing so by himself on his own. Learning about his separation, at the behest of his relatives in Idaho, he had already traveled there to get work as a miner, and within a few months he sent for his daughters. The girls' paternal grandmother, Lelia Smith, and their father's sister, their aunt by the name of Bessie Smith, would accompany them on their journey and remain, as well, in Idaho. Their father, as time would reveal, would only be around the girls occasionally and would not have a significant influence on his daughters' development. Rather, their care and upbringing was to fall on the shoulders of their grandmother, herself separated from an often-drunk husband by the last name of Comstock. She would prove to be the needed blessing to the girls, both psychologically and physically. It was under her guidance, love, and care that the girls would thrive. Through her, Mother learned to survive and to nurture others herself. She would, in turn, pass lessons of such loving care to all her children. Whereas the Bible speaks of the sins of the father being visited upon the children, surely the blessings of this grandparent were passed on to future generations. What could have easily turned out to be a dysfunctional childhood at the hands of their father, turned out instead to be remarkable development at the hands of a loving grandmother.

During a conversation I taped with my mother in 1975, she fondly recalled riding the train with her grandmother across America as a "real experience." She was only four years old at the time of the journey, but she was able to recall several things. For one thing, her Grandma had packed a suitcase full of food, since in those days there was little food service on the train that one could afford, and only a few small shops at infrequent train stops to buy provisions. She remembered in particular a huge salt shaker her grandmother had brought along and would use to "salt down" almost everything they ate. Other passengers shared both food and conversation on the long journey, and for a few brief days community was established. For girls who only knew Jamestown, this trip across America was surely eye-opening. The long journey terminated initially at the main rail station in Shoshone, Idaho. Then transferring to a local spur train, they finally arrived at the Gimlet Siding in the summer of 1915.

Helen Smith, Age 6, and Marian Smith, Age 8

Apollina Boehler

When they arrived at the Gimlet Siding—just a platform and small railroad shack with little else around it—life immediately became an effort to survive in ways that most people in today's developed countries cannot begin to imagine. I think I got a glimmer of this level of survival and what that must have been like for the two girls and their grandmother when in 1962 I served two years in Ethiopia as part of the new U.S. Peace Corps Volunteer program. There I saw first-hand what day-to-day survival required of people living on next to nothing. Although the two settings are different, the basics of what it takes to simply survive without a supporting infrastructure are common. Since their father wasn't prepared to provide a home, it fell on their relatives to initially put the girls, grandmother, and aunt up in their new-found environment.

The Gimlet Siding was a part of the Union Pacific Railroad system that opened the Wild West. Grandmother Lelia'a sister, Lida, lived near Gimlet, as did four brothers, all but one of whom was married. The whole family made their livelihood farming in the rich valleys around the now-famous Sun Valley, Idaho. For reasons he never revealed, their father gave the girls to their grandmother to raise. It was a brash, probably impulsive, act that he had not fully thought out. Fortunately, their grandmother was a person of strong character. While she had seemingly not instilled in her own son the skills of parenting, she herself would parent the two girls with great skill. Were it not for her and other relatives, Lord only knows what may have become of the two girls.

The girls, grandmother, and their aunt lived with relatives on their farm only a short time. They soon rented a small house together, a few miles away in the town of Hailey—itself then a very small hamlet. The first order of business was to find a way to bring in income. In the short run, relatives continued to provide some help in the way of basic food, clothing and supplies, but they, too, had their lives to manage on scarce resources. Fortunately, Grandmother Lelia was a skilled seamstress, and she soon began to get some occasional work. She also took in laundry and did other odd jobs, but it wasn't enough income to support two children, as well as parent on a full time basis. But, she did establish a home, even if they didn't have their own house. As it turned out, it was not her capacity to eke out a livelihood, but rather her nurturing skills that would come to mean so much to the girls. It fell on their Aunt Bessie, their father's only sister, to become the principal provider for this unusual family. Aunt Bessie was a nurse by trade and was able to provide some nursing care to those in need in and around Hailey. After living only a few months in Hailey, Aunt Bessie moved a few miles away to the nearby town of Bellevue, leaving Grandmother and the girls temporarily until she could settle into a new job she had found. As a nurse, she set up practice with the area's only physician, Dr. Raft. Together they created a small hospital to serve the valley. She did the nursing, while he provided the medical treatment. This generated most of the income for the family for all the years they lived there.

On occasion, during the winter, the girls would walk from Hailey to Bellevue to visit their aunt at the hospital. It was a distance of 5 miles, and they would pull a wooden wagon with the things they were carrying to her from their grandma, as well as their own possessions. The girls always felt secure walking by themselves during the couple of hours it took, although Mother recalls the old power plant pond known as Ghost Pond, as something to be a little leery of as a child. For no good reason, other than perhaps the name, they always made sure to run as fast as they could from one end of the pond to the perceived safer place on the other side. Nothing ever happened to them, but it was wise to be cautious even in those more genteel days. Of course, their constant story-making to see who could scare the other the most, did add to the ghostly, eerie feeling of their journey. However, the days living in Hailey didn't last long, as the girls and Grandma soon joined Aunt Bessie in Bellevue. Aunt Bessie, in the meanwhile, had met and would later marry her first husband. All of them lived in rooms at the back of the hospital.

Given the small-town nature of Hailey and the surrounding area, the period of time being 1916, and the variety of people who were in need of medical attention, living in a small hospital turned out to be a priceless experience for the girls. Mother recalled later in life that she not only learned about a variety of people, but also about the many aches and pains that required medical attention. She saw first-hand the value of pure human kindness to treat and console those with a variety of illnesses.

Mother was simply fascinated by the hospital. In her mind, it was as if it were some kind of childhood playground or science museum. She particularly remembered the operating room with its wooden table and could describe in detail the many parts of the instrument sterilizer and how it worked. There were several hospital beds—a little fact that will play significantly later in her life's story. Of particular fascination was a white granite pitcher for drawing water. In back of the hospital, next to a shed was a water pump. The girls were in charge of pumping water for daily cooking, as well as fetching water for clothes washing and to meet the various needs in the hospital. For clothes washing, Grandma heated water on an open fire and used an old, wooden corrugated wash bench, with a hand-cranked ringer on one side to extract the excess water out of the clothes. The clean, but still wet clothes would then be hung on the clothes line outdoors to dry. If you were not careful, Mother observed, in the winter the water in the pitcher would freeze if you left a slight amount of water in the bottom; then it wobbled like a top with its own center of gravity. It would be freezing cold during the winter months, but the rest of the year was mild and wonderful. There was no indoor plumbing, and of course that meant the traditional outhouse was used. But to our mother, living in the hospital was more like a wonderful dream than the odd residence others may have thought it to be. Helping the sick would become an important part of Mother's service to others later in life, and this was surely shaped living in the hospital with Aunt Bessie and being around Dr. Raft.

Aunt Bessie was both a fascinating character and an enigma. Aunt Bessie had married late in life by the standard of those days. She was 35 years old when she met and married George Archer. Mother told me one day, "When George was courting Aunt Bessie he used to bring five-pound boxes of chocolates, with 5 and 6 layers in the box, and specially coated ones on Valentine's Day." The girls delighted in sampling the chocolates, especially considering how rare such luxuries were in their life.

Aunt Bessie

I only knew and experienced Aunt Bessie when she was in her late 60s to 80s. I can't imagine she was much different in her 30s when Mother was living with her and her grandmother. Aunt Bessie was a stern woman who seemed to have suffered, unlike our mother, from the agony of just being. She had married twice, but had no children. Her manner of conversation had an aged quality. She wore her prematurely grey hair in a tight bun, dressed in dowdy, matronly clothes, and always talked and looked troubled. Knowing my mother as I did, I doubt that Aunt Bessie had much influence on Mother's character other than as a model of what not to do or be. Our mother did not share any of the negative qualities of her aunt. Don't get me wrong. Aunt Bessie was certainly an influence on Mother's life. Fortunately, it wasn't in the negative ways it could have been. From my experience with her, Aunt Bessie could just wear on you, but Mother was capable of looking beyond that negativism and taught me and my brothers and sisters to do so as well. I think this speaks to the character of our mother in what she saw and learned from others, that she accepted what was good and ignored the rest as senseless gibberish. Certainly, Aunt Bessie's contribution to our mother's survival in those early years is a fact Mother never took for granted. She always valued her aunt despite Aunt Bessie's negative attitude towards life. One of the many ways in which I admired my mother was the way she forgave those like Aunt Bessie who could have beat her down through their negative attitude. I can still hear my mother saying, "Well, that's the way she is. You never know what makes a person the way they are, so you just have to overlook some things and move on. That's just the way it is!" There was a positive side to Aunt Bessie that Mother focused on, not her faults. Mother left with us the impression that we should understand people like her. Indeed, I did come to accept Aunt Bessie for what she was, and I have certainly known others like her! Rather than expecting them to change and be more pleasant, I learned to accept them the way they are. I must say that Aunt Bessie always appreciated the way I could fix her old radio, and though grumpy, she was always nice to me. We children came to see her as a stark contrast to our mother's optimism and overall gratitude. I suppose this was, as with so many other things in life, a lesson for children that needed to be learned.

Grandma Lelia

While Aunt Bessie, with all her sternness, was a challenge, in Mothers' eyes her Grandma Lelia was just the opposite. Mother often described her life with her grandmother the way you would hope any child would talk about a grandparent or for that matter, a parent. Mother simply adored and admired her grandmother Lelia, and spoke about her with great loving affection whenever the opportunity presented itself. Mother's father allowed Grandma Lelia to adopt Mother when she was in her early teens. Strangely enough, he did not allow her sister Helen to be adopted by Grandma Lelia, creating an unsolved mystery for both girls through the remainder of their lives. The answer to that riddle died with their father; neither my mother nor her sister ever knew why he chose this path of adoption for one but not the other. No one learned what went through his mind. Was it his reaction to his wife's extramarital affair, his guilt over entering and leaving the girls' life, his aimless wandering the country-side for work, not to mention his drinking? Given an opportunity to help his girls overcome their feelings of abandonment physically and emotionally, he somehow chose the very opposite— to give one child a legal "mother," but not the other child. Neither child ever said much about it, but it surely must have weighed on their psyche in some way. Fortunately, their grandmother offered the girls equal shelter and nurturing, immense love and care, and they flourished, each in their own way. Whatever the father's emotions and intentions, there were many ways that his mother made up for his short-comings and helped the girls to grow into lovely young women.

As noted, Grandma Lelia was particularly gifted at sewing. This skill contributed to the girl's overall welfare in a very significant way besides supporting the family financially. In addition to doing seamstress work for others, she made every dress the girls wore. Mother described these dresses as universally very pretty dresses with several layers of petticoats, and a broad, hand-crocheted, four-inch lining on the bottom. Mother and her sister often talked of how these dresses made them feel special, even though they had little else materially. The clothing, hand made with loving care, not only provided cover for the girls, but assured them that appearance did matter, no matter the economic status. Consequently, our mother always felt that she was cared for, and although poor, she walked equally in the world with others of more economic wealth. That seemingly simple act of clothing the girls with some style assured a modicum of self-esteem. Having heard my wife describe how ill-suited her clothing was when her parents sent her off to college, I appreciate my mother's unerring sense of appropriate appearance. I remember how Mother, following the example of her grandmother, assured that her children went to all levels of schooling and college with wardrobes that helped them adjust and fit in. In raising her own girls she saw to it that they were well dressed. Although not a skilled seamstress herself, she hired a woman by the name Ma Hector to make dresses for her girls. These were made at the unbelievable cost of 50 cents per dress, and often included, at Ma Hector's own initiative, an identical dress for their doll. Every dress was made so that when the eldest child grew out of it, the dress went to the next in line. Our mother even, if you can imagine, insisted for a period of time that some of us "mail" our clothing home during our early college days to be personally washed and returned. It didn't take long for any of us to figure out that burdening her with such a task was far beyond the call of motherly duty—a duty she took pleasure in because she knew it made a difference in life as she had herself experienced through her grandmother. You know, sometimes it's just the little touches, no matter how small or mundane they may seem, that make the difference for each person we love. Her grandmother, my mother, and her children know what that means when it comes to rearing children. Every parent should know that life is often really in the details.

Grandma Lelia was also a great cook. A constant pot of homemade soup, wonderful sourdough biscuits, some wild game, fresh vegetables during summer from their own garden behind the hospital provided the necessities for a self-sustaining existence. This wasn't to say that times were always easy, but their Grandma had a way of meeting daily needs with very little. The sense of normalcy was what she was particularly capable of providing and it made the girls feel secure. Since their biological parents had both abandoned them physically and emotionally, it was a remarkable thing for their grandmother to achieve for them. Mother and her sister, although parentless, basically got to have a real childhood—although it would prove to be too short. Still, they had a delightful childhood thanks to Grandma Lelia and Aunt Bessie, which was critical to their security and overall character development. How many children today live with food insecurity, not to mention financial or emotional insecurity, and with varying forms of abandonment?

As to Mother's father, Hazel, as noted, he was in and out of the girls' life. He was by trade a shingler and lather, meaning that he worked repairing house roofs and constructing walls in the days long before drywall was available. Lathing involved stringing pieces of thin, narrow wood slats together with wire and securing them to the wood framing of a house. Plaster was then laid over the slats to create walls, which were smoothed later after drying, and finally painted. According to Mother, he was pretty good at it, but the work was sporadic. He supplemented lathing and shingling by working odd jobs, especially as a miner in the local ore and silver mines. When he first arrived in Idaho, he worked the Triumph, Independence, and North Star mines in the Hailey area, mining silver and lead. He never really earned much of a living, like most miners, but he had his share of experiences. Mother recalled one such experience that nearly changed their life forever: an avalanche

Soon after the children arrived from Jamestown, New York, their father was working one of the mine sites in the Hailey area. One day he had been suffering with a bout of pneumonia. As the day shift ended and the night shift was gathering, his coworkers encouraged him not to go with them to the mine because of his ill health. They would cover for him, they said. The day shift bunked down for the night, and their father moved to the boiler room to keep warm. Heating was not provided in the bunk house where the men slept and generally spent their off hours. That particular evening as he lay rolled-up in the boiler room, a huge snow storm passed through the valley and triggered an avalanche on a surrounding mountain. As the snow on the mountain roared down the valley, an entire bunk house at the North Star Mine was destroyed, and at least 13 miners were killed outright or died later. That was February 25, 1917. One of the few buildings unaffected by the avalanche was the boiler room, and through the luck of his illness, he survived. Mother always remembered how some of the miners were brought to the hospital where her Aunt Bessie worked, but none survived. Others were buried by the avalanche for days until the town folk could dig through the heavy, deep snow that sealed their doom. Already motherless, the girls were nearly fatherless as well.

Most of what Mother ever had to say about her father lacked the affection she so easily expressed for her grandmother. Between mining, roofing and lathing, and his occasional escapism into drinking, instead of helping his mother provide for the girls, he followed his own personal agenda. More than once, the little make-shift family had to receive community aid to supplement their survival. In those days, the town or county government provided some relief, rather than charitable organizations or federal assistance as in today's world. Some struggled with shame or guilt at the thought of aid. In the case of Grandmother, according to Mother's account, they accepted what help was given with great gratitude and thanksgiving for the kind generosity of others. It was a lesson Mother never forgot. She would return the generosity and kindness to her own community and to many individuals in many ways during her life time.

While the move to Bellevue was because of Aunt Bessie's new work at the hospital, there was a second necessity that prompted the move as well. This was the fact that Mother had reached, and soon Helen would be approaching, school age. Bellevue had a school and the mother was enrolled soon after the move.

Hazel Jenner Smith

Encouraged by her grandmother, schooling was a big deal to Mother. She often talked about her love for geography and history, as well as spelling and arithmetic. She especially liked math and English and excelled in both. Her only downfall, she recalled, was algebra. She had a great interest in sports—especially girls' basketball. Of course, in those days organized girl's sports were rare, but apparently in forward-thinking Idaho, girls' sports were organized and encouraged. She often talked about playing on the elementary and high school teams. The high school team made trips to many other towns to play regularly-scheduled games. She described her skill as "playing a pretty good game of basketball." For their uniform, they had a full top with short sleeves and wore bloomers with a tie string pulled at the ankles. In the latter years of her playing basketball the girls got to wear skirts down to the knees, with stockings, and they were by Mother's account, "much more comfortable."

She fondly recalled how the team got to travel from one small town to another, such as to Carey, Hailey, and others. It was winter time when they played basketball, so they were pulled by horses in a large covered sled over the snow. There was a wood-fired heater at the back of the wagon to keep them warm. She remembered that once, when they had a tournament in Hailey, it seemed to her the whole town turned out. I think that while her interest in sports fueled her competitive edge, it also fostered cooperative and genteel ways. It surely gave her a sense of joy and great pride. She earned a high school letter—a big letter "B" for the town of Bellevue. My sister Bertine neatly framed it, and displays it to this day, as a remembrance of our mother.

Bellevue High School Basketball Team
(Mother, First Row on Right)

Apparently she was a pretty good speller. At one time she achieved the honor of County Spelling Champion. I knew when I needed something spelled as a boy, I could turn to her as my walking dictionary. She once told me about a sixth-grade spelling bee she participated in. She and another girl were the last two contestants, until Mother lost out on the word, "acquaintance." She said she really knew the word, but she just couldn't remember when asked. However, she was "as happy as a clam," she said, when she was awarded a gold pencil on a long blue ribbon you could wear around your neck. Her teacher, Miss Montgomery, could not have been more proud. Many decades later when Miss Montgomery died at the age of eighty-six, Mother returned to Hailey to attend her funeral and honor her work as a teacher. She thought it a bit sad to be only one of two students to come and honor this favorite teacher. Throughout her life, our mother had a way of making sure she honored those she loved and respected for their contribution to others.

In those days, one graduated from the eighth grade and then went onto high school. As good a student as she was, Mother only got to finish the tenth grade. Nonetheless, she was one of the most educated women I would ever know.

Her enthusiasm for education made you wonder what she might have achieved had she had the kind of opportunity she so freely provided to each of her children in the way of advanced education. On a personal note, I think she could have perhaps gone on be a great intellect in her time, had not the prevailing negative attitude of society towards women in business stood in her way. Throughout her life she more than made up for her own lack of formal education with an experience degree in humanity and business. She was by all measure a master teacher to others by her actions, including everything she would teach her children about life and how to live it.

A Sudden Transition from Childhood to Married Woman

Survival took on a whole new meaning to Mother and her sister when Grandma Lelia died suddenly one fall day in 1926. It was her sister Helen's 14th birthday, and for our mother, then only herself 15, it meant instant change. She was in the 9th grade when the foundation of her security was taken away. Could she perhaps stay and be with Aunt Bessie? Would that work? And what about their father—that man who had never taken any real responsibility for his children?

It took some time to find their father who, as usual had gone his own way. He was out of touch since he was a transient in search of his next job, but eventually he was found working in Salt Lake City, Utah. He returned upon hearing of Grandma Lelia's death, attended the funeral, and gathered the girls to take them with him to Salt Lake City. Imagine going from the relative peace, quiet and security of life with their grandmother in Bellevue, Idaho, with its forests, plowed fields, and streams to move to the big city of Salt Lake City in 1926. Imagine going there with a man—their father—whom they barely knew.

Mother never said much about her days in Salt Lake City and living with her father. She recalled that it was a hot place during the summer and that her shoes would sink into the newly tarred pavement. As it was, she only stayed in Salt Lake City a short couple of months before she returned to Bellevue to live with Aunt Bessie. For her own reasons, her sister Helen stayed on and lived with her father until adulthood. The girls at that point separated, never to live under the same roof again.

Mother returned to Bellevue because it was the place she loved and Aunt Bessie needed help. Mother was never one to turn down someone in need—family or not. Aunt Bessie's husband, George, was dying of tuberculosis (TB) and Aunt Bessie could not care for him and work as well. So she asked Mother to come and help. Mother recalls that George would mostly just lie around, often in a delirious state of mind. When he was lucid, he would recount to Mother how he dreamed of sorting ore from his mining days. He had been a mining engineer—a geologist—by trade. He was sometimes found in the middle of the night deliriously sorting the ore on his bed sheets. Some times during his waking hours he would sit on the porch smoking, even with the TB ravaging his lungs. He'd fondle the samples of different rocks he had collected over the years as he had vainly attempted, as had so many others, to strike it rich. George died within months of her return. Mother had been a comfort to him and to her aunt, and she knew she had done the right thing in returning to help. This was just the part of service to many of the dying, weak, and infirm who came into her life over the years that followed.

Now without her sister, and her motherly Grandma Lelia, and in the household of the grieving and stern Aunt Bessie, Mother stayed only long enough to complete the tenth grade. This was her last year of formal education and of her days in Bellevue.

When Aunt Bessie's husband died, it seemed Mother's financial ties to her aunt also died. Aunt Bessie had her work to keep her occupied, and Mother would now need to support herself. For a short time she worked in Aunt Bessie's sister-in-law's restaurant as a waitress, where her duties also included washing clothes when needed. She made $3.00 a week plus tips; money she thought then to be really good. However, she could not, for whatever reason, continue to stay in Bellevue. Perhaps it was because her precious Grandmother was gone and there were just too many memories. Perhaps it was the absence of her sister and father, although I doubt it. Most likely it was just that she knew she had to move on to establish her own way. Knowing her as I did, her decision to "move on" was her way of saying she had to face life squarely for what it presented, rather than let circumstances paralyze her. She was always self-motivated to action. In her succinct way of facing reality, she told me about her last days in Bellevue. "I had to survive! Times were different then, you know." So, having decided to move on, the next phase of life would, as it were, pounce on her like a wild cat in the chase for its next meal. The odyssey of events that followed her last year in Bellevue would set the stage for all the years to come. Considering she started the next phase of her journey at the tender young age of just 16—a young girl and yet so much the maturing woman—it was pretty remarkable what transpired.

It was 1927, and in those days people didn't like to take care of people with cancer. It was a feared disease, equally unknown to those who had it or heard of it. A man named Lambert Lucius Langdon, then of Twin Falls, Idaho, had a wife with cancer. Her name was Myrtle Munn Langdon.

The Silmans, cousins of George Archer, Aunt Bessie's late husband, lived near Twin Falls about 75 miles south of Bellevue. This extended family of Syrian decent farmed near Gooding, Idaho, not far from Twin Falls. There were three brothers, Farris, Pete, and Dave. Dave had a family of four girls and four boys, but all the Slimans, including Dave's two brothers, lived together as one big family. Sticking together as family was a cultural habit from the old country, as well as a practical way to assure one another's survival. And the family welcomed anyone, strangers included, whenever anyone passed by the remote farm.

Now Dave Sliman was close friends with one "Bert" Lambert Lucius Langdon, and knew of his ailing wife, Myrtle. Myrtle had had cancer for nearly eight years and was finally losing her long battle with the disease. Bert needed someone to take care of his wife, because in addition to trying to make a living as a broker of hides and pelts that required traveling on occasion, he and his wife Myrtle had three children, then 14, 10 and 3. Lynn Langdon, two years younger than Mother, was the oldest boy, followed by his brother Archie, and their baby sister, Dorothy. The Langdons had had another child, Louise, their first born, who died at the age of just 9 months.

Knowing that Bert needed a care-giver for his ailing wife, and knowing Aunt Bessie, Dave Sliman suggested that perhaps Marian might want to go and work for Bert Langdon. As Mother often said later in life, "I needed a place to survive on my own," so she went to work for Mr. and Mrs. Langdon in Twin Falls in the fall of 1927.

Mother was only 16 years old, but she stepped out from what was left of the security of family to be completely on her own. And she never looked back. We can be assured that Grandma Lelia, through her loving care and instilling of self-confidence, had prepared her for that day!

Our mother came to know the first Mrs. Langdon as a sweet person and very caring mother of three. She was formerly of Tangent, Oregon, where she had met and married Bert. They moved first to Pocatello, Idaho, where her husband took a job as a hide broker, then to Twin Falls for the same kind of work, but this time on his own. She had been diagnosed with cancer a couple of years after her second son, Archie, was born. She fought bravely the little-known disease, and even had a third child during that time. For a while she had taken one of the few remedies known at that time called "Calamities Gold." It always sounded to me like some elixir sold off the back of one of those horse-drawn circus wagons by some con artist, but it did seem to have some positive effect in arresting the disease for a while. It was very expensive: $5.00 a bottle—a lot of money in those days! When she got to feeling better after four years, she stopped taking the medicine. But it wasn't long before she began to fail again. This time she didn't regain her strength and slowly began to fade to the point where she could not care for herself, let alone meet the needs of her three children and husband.

Our mother's job in the Langdon household was the general supervision of the three children and maintenance of the house, as well as her primary duty of caring for Mrs. Langdon. She was paid $8 a week plus room and board. She recalls how she would frequently dress the wound on Mrs. Langdon's breast. The cancer kept eating down and further into her breast cavity. Her arm would swell, and Mother would clean the wound with alcohol and put a clean dressing on it daily. In these moments the two women shared thoughts on everything in life—one the dying mother and the other the younger woman just starting out. During those conversations, they tried to avoid the mention of death. But death did come at the age of 35 for Myrtle. Our mother had come in the fall of 1927 and by February of the next year, with her patient gone, she was once again at a crossroads. Where to go and what to do?

Bert Langdon and First Wife, Myrtle

Mother's marriage to Bert Langdon was a marriage of convenience. She said more than once, "He needed someone to take care of the children, and I needed a place to live." There probably is no better summation of life's necessity than those few words. But that didn't mean that they did not come to love one another through the years that followed. What began as a marriage of convenience and survival eventually turned into one of mutual respect and love.

In the early days of their marriage her role was clear: raising three children, one only slightly younger than herself, and each one reeling from the loss of their biological mother. It's hard to imagine this new 17-year-old "mother" managing 15- and 11-year-old boys and a four-year-old girl. She once said of that experience, "It wasn't the easiest thing in the world, but their father made them mind, and we got along." None of the children ever spoke disparagingly of her mothering in the years that followed. She was a natural at mothering, as I can surely attest, but I am certain that her own up bringing under the care of her loving grandmother played a large role in her nurturing skills. She always said, "I loved mothering and would have had more children had your father agreed."

Lambert Lucius Langdon, or "Bert" as he was called by all, was an honest, trusted man. In his bachelor days in Oregon, as described by his uncle George, he "was a rambler, gambler, and had a way with the women." Long, tall, and lean, he struck a handsome image as a young man. He was the son of Lucius Lambert Langdon and Emma Louise LaFrancis, who were pioneers of the old Wild West. His mother was a women's temperance leader later in life; his father, at and early age, was a victim of vigilantes. Although this is the story of our mother, a brief sidetrack into her husband's history is worthwhile since it sheds light on the times, the people, and influences on our father's life, as well as our mother's life.

Mother and Father Married, 1928

Grandpa Lucius, our father's father, homesteaded in Oregon near the town of Prineville. He married Emma Louise LeFrancis in Illinois, and with two of his brothers came west around 1880 to do ranching. Lucius acquired 160 acres under the Federal Land Grant program. He was homesteading and cattle ranching on a nice, forested piece of property that stood high above a valley near Prineville. He had a neighbor by the name of A. H. Crooks, whose daughter had just married a man by the name of Stephan J. Jory in 1882. Crooks wanted to provide for his daughter and new son-in-law, and so he planned to divide the property he was homesteading into a separate 80-acre parcel that the newlyweds would live on and work. The problem was that he was taking 40 acres as his own, and what was legally (according to a subsequent court case) 40 acres of our grandfather's land. It was more likely a misguided error on his part than malicious intent, but he didn't heed repeated warnings about the problem he was creating. This misunderstanding eventually led to bad blood between Crooks, Jory, and our grandfather.

The dispute over boundaries went on for some time. Our grandfather is reported to have said to Crooks in a final warning, "If you continue to try and blaze your new fence past that tree stump over there on my property, there will be an account to pay." Crooks, along with his son-in-law, continued to blaze a fence line past the tree onto Grandpa's property, and there was indeed a price to pay. After some heated words one fateful day, shots were exchanged, and Grandfather killed both Crooks and Jory and went home, apparently feeling nothing else was to be said or done. However, the local Prineville sheriff, having heard of the incident, soon showed up at Grandfather's cabin, and as Grandfather started to ride away on a white horse, the sheriff identified himself. "Hey, Langdon, it's Sheriff Blakely!" They knew one another, so Grandfather stopped, and then he and the sheriff went inside to talk some things over while having dinner. The sheriff noted in an article that appeared in an Oregon newspaper some years later that it was a congenial conversation, and, "By the way, Mrs. Langdon is quite the cook." The sheriff and Grandfather agreed he would surrender himself and stand for trial since he felt he was justified in defending his land after repeated warnings to Crooks and Jory.

As part of their agreement, Grandfather was supposed to be incarcerated in the jail located at the county seat, The Dalles, Oregon, and await trial. But, given the lateness of the day, he would spend the night in Prineville first. Prineville, being a small town, didn't have a jail. So the sheriff chained Langdon to a bed in the only local hotel. That night, ten or twelve men overpowered the lone guard—later reported to be part of the vigilantes—outside the hotel room, and broke in and shot Grandfather to death. It was further reported that the next day some of the same men found Grandfather's hired hand, named Harrison, who had had nothing to do with the incident, and hanged him from a bridge in town. These incidents began a ten-year period of vigilantism in which numerous others in the Prineville area were killed. There is some speculation that Grandfather's killing was merely the beginning of this group's control of the flow of cattle and sheep in the area. The fact that the Langdon land stood on the crossroads of the movement of cattle out of the valley was significant. Of most keen interest to me and subsequent generations of Langdons, other than the incident itself, was the fact that Grandma Emma Louise was pregnant with our still-to-be-born father. He was born six months after the shootings. Personally, as Lambert's last offspring, I call that a two-time-close-call! Having researched this story myself, I found it very curious to learn that Grandmother Emma and Mrs. Crooke remained friends long after the shooting. It's apparent that in those pioneering days difficult times forged strange bedfellows in both death and survival. Such stories speak volumes about a time and place that seems so removed from what we experience today; just as our current times will be seen as different for others a hundred years from now. As it was, for our grandparents and our parents, a different time from ours, it is not always that easy to judge why they did what they did.

Our father spent most of his youth in Tangent, Oregon. It was there that he met and married Myrtle Munn on December 2, 1911. The reader might make note of the year, 1911, as that is the year of birth of the subject of this book—our mother. Lambert and Myrtle bore four children: Louise, an infant who died at nine months; Lynn who was born on October 5, 1913; Archie, born May 10, 1917; and finally Dorothy, born January 8, 1924. The family, before Dorothy's birth, moved from Oregon to Idaho around 1922.

When Father's first wife died of cancer in February, 1928 he had no family support system in the town of Twin Falls, although he certainly knew plenty of people who were more than willing to help a widower. However, at that time in his business he had to travel widely and often to make a living. One day, as the story goes, he and Marian Orena Smith, who had so diligently taken care of his wife and children, sat down to talk over his situation and hers. She could, of course, no longer stay in the house she had been providing care in, for that would not be acceptable to her or the community. People in those days would have talked most viciously about such an arrangement between any man and woman, let alone a new widower and his hired help. In what seemed more like a business discussion than certainly dating and getting to know one another, they decided that as Mother put it, "We liked one another," and "I needed a home and those kids needed a mother, so we got married four months later." It was, in every sense of the account she gave to me in a taped interview in 1976, what she characterized as a "Marriage of convenience." The nineteen years of marriage that followed proved to have met both parties' needs, and they did come to love and respect one another. Together, they had five more children, and always spoke highly of one another. Considering they were 28 years apart in age, it was a remarkable union. Certainly, one of the lessons I learned early in life was that age doesn't have to make as much a difference in relationships as does the mutual respect and conduct that bridges that difference.

Father in Front of the Warehouse

Before his marriage to Myrtle Munn, Bert had done some cowboying for a while up in Wyoming, and one of his acquaintances was reported to have gone on to be an outlaw of some repute, but we never learned who it was. His cowboying was short-lived, as he didn't seem to find the work economically satisfying. Thus, Bert began the business that would be his life's work as a hide broker. He would wander throughout Oregon and make arrangements to buy horse and cow hides from a variety of sources and then sell them to traveling salesmen, known as Drummers. Drummers were agents who traveled the territory looking for these unusual commodities to sell to tanning operations on the east coast. When he moved to Idaho with his family, Bert expanded his brokering of hides when he came to know a person representing the Bissinger Company, located in Boise, Idaho. He started buying cow hides from local meat markets, such as the Central Market in Twin Falls, from the Independent Meat Company, as well as directly from various farmers and ranchers throughout the Magic Valley region of southern Idaho. He performed a preliminary "salting" of the hides, and when he had enough, they were trucked to the offices of the Bissinger Company located in Boise, Idaho or Troutdale, Oregon. From there, they were put into railway cars and shipped to tanning companies, such as the one located in Tonawanda, New York. The tanning company made leather goods of various sorts. Bert was widely known and respected by all who met and had business dealings with him. As Mother said, "Your dad's word was like gold, and he lived in a time when your word was as good as a signature on a piece of paper."

Our mother had apparently not gone out with many boys or men before meeting our father. Since she was only 16 when she went to work for Bert and his ailing wife, she probably hadn't dated much. When they did get married on May 20, 1928, there wasn't a honeymoon because kids and the business had to be attended to.

Overall, Mother always said she and our father, "...got on real well. Your dad and I never had a serious time. The only serious time was over his occasional drinking. He would not give it up, and might have lived longer had he not drank. But, he was always good to me and you kids." As she went on to say on the topic of drinking, "They say that drinking gives you an appetite, but I can't see it. It's an excuse! It's a way to escape!" She never drank any alcohol. I think the lessons of her father's drinking, her grandfather's drinking, and her own husband's drinking proved strong reminders of the ills of alcohol.

The early years for her, her husband, and the three children were economically tough. Although it was the beginning of the Depression, they were getting by better than many. Most people had almost nothing and scraped by with government support and public food handouts. Our parents shared with others what they did have, and Mother was thankful to God for the blessing of a good husband and her new family.

In the days before their permanent business really got going, Mother recalls how they often traveled to Boise, Idaho, the capital city, to get loads of vegetables that they would then resell in order to supplement their family income. They had a big, flat-bed Chevy truck with 4-foot iron sides and a tail gate that could be placed down and up as needed for loading or unloading things. They would load the truck as full as possible with all kinds of vegetables they bought at the Chinese Gardens in Boise. There were huge heads of lettuce, turnips, tomatoes, and onions, and they were placed in wooden crates. As they drove their way back to Twin Falls, they made a run through towns like Carey, Hailey, and Buhl. People would buy right off the truck the fresh vegetables that were rare in the outlying areas. At that time, the Treasure and Magic Valley areas of Idaho were not the vast farming lands that were to come after water was dammed and canals were constructed to form one of the largest irrigated tracts in the world. Our parents would sell lettuce for four cents a head and supplement their own food supply. If people, by the way, didn't have money to pay for the vegetables, our parents traded for everything from chickens, to sheep pelts, or old used car batteries and anything else of value. Certainly getting the vegetables was important, but it seemed what you brought to one another in the way of communication from the outside world was equally important.

Dorothy, their only daughter at the time, would go along with them, and she remembers well what that was like. Before they had their own first child together, they devoted the time to getting to know and respect each other as man and wife, father, and step-mother. But there was more than vegetables to be hauled in those early days.

Mother and Father also traveled extensively throughout the southern region of Idaho and into the northern parts of Utah and Nevada. They would travel east over to Abilene and to the Utah line to pick up peaches and tomatoes to resell and supplement their income. As they were traversing west back home to Twin Falls they sold the produce to people on their way just as they did from Boise. In doing so, they met and knew people in virtually every small hamlet throughout the region. Father had a way about him of meeting people and readily making life-long friends. He loved singing, and was a fan of Burl Ives, including in his repertoire songs like "The Erie Canal" and "Home on the Range." He loved community theatre and was apparently an accomplished actor in his own right. It was one of those legacies he passed to more than one of his children. But it was his love of card playing throughout life that probably gave him the most pleasure (other than fishing), if not some rebuke from our mother. With an El Roi Tan cigar cuddled between his cheek and teeth, his large Stetson hat cocked on his head, and a grin on his face like Buffalo Bill Cody, he was the picture of a serious gambler. And he was a pretty good "snooker player" as well.

Of the many places Mother remembered traveling most, it was especially to the little hamlet of Stravell, Idaho. Stravell was essentially just a hotel in the early pioneer days and still was at that time. It was probably an early stagecoach point, which explains why the hotel was out in the middle of absolutely nowhere. It was merely an oasis in the long journey made from distant points in Nevada up into Idaho. It seems that the owner of the hotel, a Mr. Sours, was, in addition to being the hotel proprietor, the one and only local bootlegger in the area. The state of Idaho had been the sole source of the hard stuff, as they called it, until national Prohibition banned all liquor distribution and sales. Nonetheless, Father would take a few select orders for the hard stuff from various personal friends in the Twin Falls area, like his friend Sam Elrod, for a keg or two of Sours' good old moonshine. Mind you, this was for personal friends and not for sale to just anyone. Don't get me wrong, I don't think Father or Mother ever thought of themselves as bootleggers, but it wasn't like they didn't participate in the supply chain. Sours wouldn't let anyone, including our father, go with him to the moonshine still that was hidden in the desert sage brush. But you could order as many kegs as you wanted and he'd have them ready upon your arrival at the hotel. So Father and Mother typically had orders from several of their friends. They would place the 5-gallon, charcoal-lined wooden kegs in the truck and bury them under a load of cow and horse hides that surely no one would bother to move and search under. Had any member of law enforcement ever ridden in the truck with them he might well have wondered what that sloshing sound was as they drove back and forth over those bumpy gravel and washboard-dirt roads.

Mother told us countless stories about the people they met along the way, and the many they made life-long friends of and saw over and over. Near the hamlet of Bridge, for example, there was a family with 15 children. Oftentimes, our parents would stay the night with this family. There was never a question of sharing good food with visitors and friends. People extended themselves in those days and made you feel part of the family, in the same way that the Slimans had earlier done for Mother and her grandmother. Perhaps this was because of the long distance and times between seeing old friends and welcoming strangers. As a result, people were more dependent on one another, trusting of a stranger and therefore in those days more welcoming.

Deep into the Depression, Mother and her husband, now of three years, had their own first child. Born in 1931, her name was to be Lucille LaFrancis, named after, we are told, one of dad's old girl friends, combined with the maiden name of our grandmother, Emma Louise LaFrancis. Lucille was born at home in a house our parents rented on 2nd Street West in Twin Falls. The house was not big enough for the expanding family, so they later rented another, larger house on 3rd Street North. They rented the house from a Mr. Johnson for $15 a month. Mr. Johnson rented the home to them because he knew Father, trusted him, and knew they would really take good care of the house and property. Banks were closed on account of the Depression, but our father always had good credit in town.

Just two years later, their second child, Bertine Lynnette, was also born at home, this time in another rental located in the 500 block of 2nd Avenue West. Since she was born at home, the doctor decided to spend the night with the family just to be certain no complications would go unnoticed. Imagine such a thing happening today with a physician! Mother recalled how she paid six cents a yard for "oaten" flannel—the sacks that oats had been packed in—to make Bertine's diapers. Oaten-sacks would continue to be the source of diapers for all of us kids. Mother wasn't averse to using odd materials for the purpose at hand. Years later I remember the dish towels she made from used flour sacks, with labels once clearly printed, but fading after years of use. When I got married, she gave us a stack of those dish towels which we used for many years. She was never one to be caught short of anything she liked, so she had boxes of the old flour sacks waiting for use until the day she died. Stashing things away, like some squirrel preparing for the winter months, became one of her trademarks. Whether driven by innate practicality or shaped by years of being without the basics, she never wasted anything, living out the adage, "Waste not, want not."

Mother and Father's first male child was born in 1935. He got his name in the most unusual way. Unlike their other children who were born at home, he was born in Mrs. Woods' maternity home on July 12, 1935. His proud older sister, Lucille, all excited at having a new brother proceeded to run about the neighborhood announcing that she had a new "baby buzzer!" At least that was what it sounded like since she wasn't quite clearly pronouncing "brother." It must have been her excitement at the time, because there is no record of any speech defect, and she was about 8-years old at the time. Well, the name stuck and he was forever called "Buzz." His name of record is actually Lambert Lucius Langdon Jr., named after his father and grandfather, but he and everyone else preferred, for perhaps obvious reasons, the less formal name of Buzz. Even his formal name came about with an unusual timing twist, as did the naming of all the Langdon children by their unconventional parents.

When Buzz was born, no birth certificate was immediately issued. It seems that the doctor and the parents just didn't quite get around to the necessary documentation in a timely manner. It was only when my mother went to register our brother for school at the age of six that they even noted the problem; after all, he already had the name Buzz. But a formal birth certificate was required by the school, so Mother called our family doctor, Dr. Drake—always our family physician—and told him she needed a birth certificate. No problem for him, so he asked what name she wanted on the certificate. This came up so suddenly that she had not really discussed it with her husband. The doctor suggested he be named with Bert's legal name with a Jr. on the end. Mother readily agreed, and so it was. He was legally Lambert Lucius Langdon, Jr. It turns out, however, that Father wasn't so pleased when Mother returned home and told him the news. He never liked the name himself, having had it passed to him in a reverse order of his father's first and middle name, Lucius Lambert. That's was why Father called himself Bert. But it was too late! As far as Buzz's name went, Father had to accept the legal name that was now on the birth certificate. Never mind, because all that was really important was that he finally had a birth certificate, and he was forever our brother Buzz. Having a name you are comfortable with is really important, and it was a gift to us to have had parents who were not all hung up with formality of given names. You could take on a nickname, if desired, that suited your perception of yourself. You'll see this informality again and again as you learn other things that went on in this fascinating family when it came to naming each child, and so many other aspects of our life with our parents.

Our sister Lorraine Lyla, the eighth child, was born on August 9, 1936, thirteen months after brother Buzz. For some time, the story goes, Mother would humorously pass off Lorraine and Buzz as twins. But it didn't go very far with those who knew our family, so she gave up on the charade. Father named Lorraine, a fact that Mother learned only as she was leaving the hospital. This time Father got to the legal designation before Mother did. Seems on the way home from the hospital, he turned to Mother and announced that the baby's name was registered as Lorraine. It was only later that Mother discovered that Lorraine was the name of a girlfriend he fancied in his bachelor days.

Lorraine was the only one of us children born in a hospital. It seems the only reason for this was that Mother went to the hospital, at the urging of the family doctor, with some pains six weeks before she was due to deliver. She stayed there for three days under observation with a severe pain in her side. Dr. Drake, fearing something more major than mere pressure from the baby against her mother's side—more likely against her spine—decided to induce delivery. At close to midnight of that day Lorraine was born. Mother recalls that she was the smallest of her children at birth and that she was really, really red. The cost of her week's stay in the hospital was $21. Apparently, as the story goes, the hospital staff got together and decided that they would charge Mother $3.00 a day for her maternity care. Can you imagine that happening today? While eliminating the deep struggles the average person undergoes, have we given up some simple and more flexible ways?

Lucille, Bertine, and Danny were all born at home. Buzz, born in a maternity home and Lorraine in a hospital were the only two born in conventional institutions as we know them today. When she was 75, Mother told me in a conversation that, "I really had an easy time delivering children on average, and I would have had more if your father (already approaching himself 60) would have allowed it."

It might not have gone without notice that most of the Langdon children's first or middle names have the letter "L" associated with them. Combined with some kind of unwritten competition between our parents to see who would name each child, it's no wonder there resulted a menagerie of names you don't commonly find today.

Thus, we have Lucius Lynn, Lucille LaFrancis, Bertine Lynnette, Lambert Lucius Jr. (Buzz), and Lorraine Lyla. Only Archie (Archibald) David, Dorothy Jane, and yours truly, Danny G., escaped the "L" brand as part of our first or middle name. Father had this thing, it seems, with the initials L. L. from his father's and his own name—Lucius and Lambert—such that a single or double L would be branded whenever possible into his children's names. We suspect that in naming Archie, Dorothy, and Danny, Father had a momentary lapse and was persuaded to forego the traditional naming convention for his children. In the case of naming Archie, for instance, it was the will of dad's mother, Myrtle Munn, whose second husband's last name was Archibald that must have been the influencing factor. She was visiting from Oregon at the time of the birth of the child who would become Archie. I am not sure where Dorothy's name originated. As to my own name, I asked my mother about it when I was about 55 years old. To me, her answer was a classic and spoke volumes about the simple way she saw the world. "Well," she said, "That's the way it was meant to be: Danny G." I always especially liked that answer and I loved my mother even more for having expressed it that way. It told me that I didn't really have to be anything other than exactly who I was. Not a bad lesson to learn about yourself. At her funeral, I took the opportunity to thank her one last time for the gift of the special name she chose for me, as our parents did in their own special way for each child. Each of us, throughout separate lives, really cherished and liked the name we were given by our parents as oddly, humorously, or even deceitfully it may have come to be. Surely our names, as with so many traits and peculiarities came with the same love that would forever be their special form of parenting skills.

It's pretty common in combined families, such as was ours from two different mothers, that parents or children use the parental or sibling prefix designation of "step" when referring to one another. Thus, it would be stepbrother, stepsister, stepmother, or stepfather. Our parents never did and made a special point of always referring to their children as their son or daughter. In turn, as children we referred to one another as my brother or sister; never, never using the prefix "step." As a result, you knew that everyone in the family was your equal. Of course, it took some explaining at times when people learned that you had a brother that was two years younger than your mother or there was, as in my case, a brother 25 years my senior. Or that our father was born in 1882, when most people my age had grandparents who were born at that time. Then there was the fact that I had a niece that was two years older than I was. Personally, I've always liked explaining that our father was 28 years older than our mother and watching people's jaw drop at the sheer thought of it. Frankly, age is far less a deal than society make of it. You know it really depends on the person, the individual's situation, time and circumstances. When I think of my mother's time and place, it all makes perfect sense to me and to my brothers and sisters, so we never apologize and indeed take great pride in our family's heritage. It's nice to be a little, if not significantly different from others.

To ease the financial burden during the Depression, and for a number of years thereafter, our parents left behind the house they rented at the time, packed up the family, and went to the mountains to live for the entire summer. That's right, while school was out we went to the mountains to live off the land for three months. This was not, however, totally some fun summer vacation time or little trip to the country or a camp ground for a week or two. It involved packing all the family's possessions and living in the woods as if it were home. Precious rent and related living expenses could be saved this way. While moving to the mountains was depression-driven, I suspect my father saw it also as a wonderful opportunity to fish, fish, fish. Bertine was only three weeks old when the family went for the first time to the Sawtooth Mountains on the Little Wood River, not far from Aunt Bessie and Grandma's original home near Hailey. It would be a trek that would be repeated every year for slightly more than a decade. Not even Bertine's bout with "Scarlatina," known better as Scarlet Fever, would stand in the way of this annual trip. These trips created wonderful memories for us Langdons.

Camping on the Little Wood River

Living in the outdoors was sheer delight, although I am sure, a lot of work for our parents. Living amongst trees and beside the creeks and streams for three months at a time was a return to nature; we had a kind of pioneer experience in the early thirties and mid-forties. There was nothing quite like eating trout you caught that day, combined with some local fresh farm eggs at ten cents a dozen, local bacon, and hash browns cooked over an open camp fire. We hiked, we slept out under the trees at night; we gathered around camp fires, collected bugs, whittled flutes from willow trees and ran into all sorts of wild life, including rattlesnakes. There was nothing quite like listening to the sound of the creek that we were camped near, and the rustle of the trees, as a gentle breeze blew through camp just before a light rain storm. Then there was the morning dew that hung on the tent begging for the sun to dry it out and warm your body so you could crawl from under the warm blankets into a new day's experiences. But among all the things we enjoyed, the most fun of all was the fishing. A movie of a few years ago, "A River Runs Through It," almost captured the scenic beauty of how wonderful those days were, especially fishing with my brothers. Our lives reflected the same pure beauty of the mountains and the fondness we all had for fishing. The strong feelings of brotherly and sisterly love that grew while camping would make a movie of its own.

Father was an avid fisherman! His skill bordered on sheer artistry as he extended his fishing line in perfect rhythm in that swirling motion that only an accomplished fly fisherman can. He always seemed to catch his 24 Cutthroat or Rainbow Trout limit in a day or perhaps two limits. Topped by his Stetson hat, with a wood-reed creel around his shoulder and resting on his waist, he placed the fish he caught on the sweet-smelling grass he had pulled from the meadow. It wasn't unusual for him to go out both morning and evening, fishing to the edge of moonlight.

One morning, while fishing, Father noticed that his ever-present, prized gold signet ring was missing. He rarely took the ring off, even to wash his hands. He remembered seeing it while drinking coffee that morning, before he set off for his favorite fishing holes. He figured he had lost it within the last 75 yards of fishing since he hadn't gone very far that morning. How would he ever find it? He summoned the whole family around, and we began to search both the stream and the surrounding bank. It was like trying to find the proverbial needle in a haystack. Finally, in some kind of desperation he decided to stretch one of the camp canvas tarps across the stream where he thought the ring was most likely to be. It was an area just above a swirling deep fishing hole. It was hard to see very far down into the hole because of its depth, even with the shining sunlight that glistened overhead at high noon. Using the canvas as a kind of makeshift dam merely diverted some of the rapid flowing water to another path, but it did allow one to see more clearly into that now-shallower hole. And there, deep in the fishing hole, he found his cherished ring, glistened by the sun's rays. I think it was a minor miracle that the ring was found, but it became part of the Langdon memory of adventures on the Little Wood River.

Mother was every bit as skilled at fishing as Father. To see her in hip-boots and a light brown cotton shirt and, with her casting line and fly ready to haul back any fish that tugged the line was a thing of beauty. There was only one time that she told me later that fishing caused her any concern. One early morning she was fishing on Mall Creek, just a little back of the Little Wood River. Father had said he would watch the kids that evening because he loved it that she enjoyed fishing as much as he did. As was often the case, guests were at the camp site. They included George Vantilberg, who used to be our barber, and other close friends, Mr. and Mrs. Zeek Jones. Zeek sold Buicks at Browning Auto in Twin Falls. Mother loved Buicks— she must have owned later in life at least a half dozen, each with more fancy chrome than the previous one. Having guests wasn't unusual, since any number of people came through the camp as they fished the river, or were, themselves, camped nearby to make ends meet. Because immigrant Basques, originally from Spain, were prominent in Idaho tending the huge flocks of sheep that wintered the hills and valleys of Idaho, they sometimes stopped by. In general, the Basques kept to themselves, although Father knew many of them well.

On this particular day, Mother was fishing right along on Mall Creek, checking her luck at each fishing hole for five or ten minutes, and doing quite well, as she recalls. She had a kind of special style in her fishing method; one that I seemed to have inherited. When she caught a fish and could feel it nibbling the bait and hook on the end of the fishing line, she would give her fishing rod a quick jerk with her wrist, letting her arm arch back swiftly to shoulder height. This quick jerk caused the fish line, hook, and fish to fly out of the water, hopefully landing the fish on the creek bank just behind. Thus, as you waded into any hole in the river, you first scouted the terrain just behind you for a great spot to land the fish you were sure was there. You can then easily retrieve the fish as it flops on the rocky bank or in the sword grass. Even if your fish ends up in a bush or tree, it is better there than back in the water where the ever-squirming fish can wiggle off your hook, causing you to be disgusted and disappointed. Of course, sometimes the fishing line did dangle from a bush or tree, and the squirming fish wrangled its way off the hook—causing perhaps the utterance of some cussword. Still, "jerking" was the technique preferred by some in the family, including our mother.

This time as she performed the jerking, hip-turning action to land a fish on her line she slipped on some mossy rocks and fell flat on her stomach on a sandbar. "Flat as a fritter," she told me many years later. Now this would not have been such a notable occurrence, except that she was eight months pregnant with me! Her matter of a fact description of this story continued as she said, "I lay there for a while, got up, got my fish, and I went back to camp." Note that part of the phrase, "Got my fish!" She went on, "The others (in the camp) had caught hardly anything. Your father felt so proud that I had caught so many, while the others had not." But, the story doesn't end there!

As was usual, that evening Mother fixed dinner for everyone. After dinner they had a huge camp fire and sat around and talked well into the darkness of a pleasant summer evening. George Vantilberg and the Joneses had to leave to go home, so the family bedded down around 11:00 p.m. for the night. Some slept in under a large, canvas army tent, while others had beds in the back of a big flat truck with iron sides. A canvas tarp over the top of the truck kept the rain out. Father had made the fairly comfortable beds by constructing iron frames which he had welded with springs taut over them, and laid stuffed mattresses. We remember them being okay to sleep on. But it was the smell of that canvas, especially when the hot sun beat on it, that we remembered most. It's an oily pungent smell, as if old railroad wooden ties were soaked in some preservative. Those in the military of some years past know what this unique smell was like and how it penetrated your nostrils until you fell into a deep sleep at night brought on by the chilly forest air and the lingering camp fire smell. If it rained or morning dew was present, that smell was slightly sharper only because of the water that was repelled by the canvas surface.

That night, Mother woke up in the middle of the night recounting that she "Didn't feel so good." She sat alone at the edge of the camp fire for a while until there were only shimmering coals. Father was awakened by her absence and came out to find out what was going on. They poked at the fire with sticks to stir the flames up and talked for a while before going back to bed. She tells how she had terrible chills and shook like a leaf during much of the rest of the night. But she did eventually fall asleep and was okay in the morning. Given that excitement, she said that Danny was the easiest delivery of the five children she and Dad had between them. I was born a month after her fall on the river bank, and like nearly all their children, was not delivered in a hospital. I was born in a warehouse in Twin Falls, Idaho on November 16, 1938. Isn't it interesting that to this day, on a rare occasion, I get chills in the middle of the night and shake like a leaf? Wonder where that comes from?

For cooking in the outdoors, Father made a huge iron contraption, much like a charcoal grill but bigger, with four legs that fit sturdily on the ground, under which plenty of wood could be gathered for a fire. He used rims from an old pioneer wagon wheel that probably had seen its way from Missouri or somewhere else as the pioneers traveled the Oregon Trail across Idaho to Oregon. The original Oregon Trail runs right through Twin Falls; it is the street our house and business warehouse were on. He welded some legs of angle iron onto the rims. He then used solid bars of iron to form a grate that was firmly welded in place, lasting through years of camping and picnics. He also built a boiler to heat water and a washtub to do the clothes washing. With the soft water from the river, Mother said, "We had the whitest clothes you ever saw." They used an old frying pan that now adorns the wall of my kitchen, and had lots of other skillets, pots and pans. The fry pan had once belonged to an old miner, and Dad had picked it up for a song—probably quite literally, as he often serenaded others with familiar verses of the old Wild West. A specially-built storage cabinet kept both the cooking items and food that Dad purchased once a month while he retrieved mail in connection with his hide-brokerage business. For ten cents you could buy a dozen eggs, a pound of bacon, or loaf of bread. We were living the great life in the wilderness, but some necessities required an income, so Father kept up the brokerage business in hides while still camping.

One of the other favorite "contraptions"—a word my mother used often later in life when she could not quite remember the name of an item—was a Dutch oven Father made. He loved to make sourdough bread, but it required an oven to cook it. He would take coals from the constantly-burning camp fire to surround the Dutch oven. Then, he'd put his specially formulated dough in, cover it and let it simmer there. With some beans and ham in an adjacent cast-iron pot (also still in my possession), potatoes, and freshly-caught fish, what more could you want? Of course, there was also fresh game to be had like pheasant, grouse, sage hens, and the like, but Father was always sure to take only what was needed. He and Mother were boiled with anger one summer when a group of strangers came up from Burley to the creek and hunted the grouse to the point that they never saw them again in that region. I believe my parents were essentially conservationists, even though, much as the American Indians did, they literally were living off the land. Perhaps it's the recognition that the land helped them survive that made them respect it all that much more. Later two sisters each married a rancher and a farmer respectively—men of the land. I am certain that the years at the Little Wood River taught these sisters environmental lessons vital to their livelihoods.

What I can personally remember of those days camping for the summer is somewhat limited by my then-young age, but I certainly remember enough to be nostalgic at a moment's notice. I was six when summer camping ended because of our aging Father's illness. I do remember the pure enjoyment and comfort of it all. The smell of fresh clean air as mountain dew settled on the wild grasses. Of times running up and over the creek, and wandering in the meadows and between the trees, hand-in-hand with my sisters and brothers. It was a time with good food and good cheer. We had a three-legged dog named "Blackie," named after his silk-like fur. He would follow us down to the stream and sit there as we fished and move dutifully when we leapfrogged from one fishing hole to the next. As children, we always had plenty of cats and a dog or two to keep us company, tagging along as we went about town or ventured to the canyon near our house to play or fish. The dogs provided companionship and a sense of security from their presence or by protectively growling at any stranger or animal that might approach. Each of my dearly loved dogs passed away after years of dutiful companionship while I was off at college and in the Peace Corps. I was deeply saddened by their passing. I can still remember each one that slept at the bottom of my bed, licked my face, or scampered ahead of me as I explored the world of my youth.

I still remember vividly the thrill of catching my first fish on the Little Wood River. The very first time I saw a fish on the end of my line I immediately became suspicious, since the fish was lying there limp and dead on its side. I had enough experience from watching my parents' fish to know a struggling fish on the end of your line from a dead one lying there motionless in the pool of water. I suspected someone—probably my father—had tied that fish on my line. So that was never the real official "First Fish I Caught Myself." When I did finally catch a fish all by myself, I still remember the smiles on my parents' faces when I came around the camp fire and showed them the wiggling fish at the end of my fishing pole. To me it's one of those special remembrances of wonderful times and loving parents. Imagine getting to spend summer after summer with your family camping out for three months in surroundings that were dream-like! Perhaps that is why I choose to live today in the midst of a forest, high on a mountain that overlooks a wondrous lake. It takes me back to that time and place, as well as to many other experiences of growing up in Idaho with my parents.   Of course, looking back at those times on the Little Wood River makes me nostalgic, but I recognize that sometimes we did things that were a little unusual. On the not-so-unusual side, we spent lots of time making birch whistles from the local tree limbs that surrounded the river. They could be made to have varying sounds from deep bass to high-pitched sounds. Others were made of the abundant weeping willow trees along the creek banks, and these, too, each gave their unique sound. You learned to carefully remove the bark, much as the Indians must have, then notch the wood and slide the bark back on to produce a fine whistle. It could provide hours of enjoyment making and playing with it. We would run a competition to see who could make the best whistle, and usually our brother Buzz won. But there was another competition that makes me wonder whatever went through our minds. It's obvious that we kids had too much time on our hands.

Apparently, one of us got the bright idea of having a contest to see which one would get the most mosquito bites over a twenty-four-hour period. My sister Lorraine claims that she was the winner of that unusual contest since her blood type seems to have been "type M," for mosquito. We itched and scratched all night with those bites. Be that as it may, it seemed those days on the creek were always filled with good times; those memories warm us all to this day.

By the time I was born in 1938, and all the family members that were to be the Langdon clan were in place, the effects of the Depression had pretty much waned, and our parents' business would change as well. Up until this time, Father had mostly centered the business on the brokerage of hides, wool, furs and pelts. Times were changing with the approach of the Second World War. Mother's recollections about life during the remainder of her time with our father are best summarized in her descriptions many years later of how they established a permanent business located in our hometown of Twin Falls, Idaho. Up until that time, the business had literally been a virtual brokerage business run out of our father's mind, with no place to actually call or to go to if you were a customer. She recounted to me the events leading up to establishing the physical location of the business in a taped interview recorded when she was in her 70s. We have to backup our time line to 1934.

The evolution of the family business to a permanent location actually started in 1934. The Depression was still on, but some of the banks had reopened after a long closure. Mother and Father were renting a house on 3rd Street North, and in turn had rented the upstairs to a couple to further help make ends meet. Father had decided it was time to have a warehouse where he could accumulate and conduct the hide, wool, fur, and pelt business. With a permanent warehouse, he would not have to travel so much. Up to that time, he relied on his clients to store the hides until he would pick them up on a regular basis and prepare them as needed prior to shipment to the tannery. Having their own warehouse to store the hides would make it possible to accumulate a large quantity of hides and prepare them more efficiently and conveniently for shipment. This was not, as you might well imagine, a kind of business that many people would find that pleasing to undertake, nor did neighbors want to live near a business where hides were stored. Fortunately, the warehouse he eventually obtained was located in an area of few houses and therefore few complaints. I can personally assure you that when you walked or drove by the business, you smelled an odor roughly akin to that of a dairy farm or sugar beet processing plant. But, this was even worse. Or imagine a dead animal that has lain in the warmth of the sun for a few days, and you'll get the idea of what pungent smell means.

As kids, we got used to the smell, the flies, the overall appearance of stacks of hides and pelts hanging from various places in the warehouse, and wool and furs in other locations. Most of our friends, oddly enough, got used to the appearance and smell as well, or at least we thought they did. This either attested to their loyalty as childhood friends, or probably, more likely, their simple desire to play in our interesting domain with us; besides, we all knew the smell and the general look of the place to be part of our livelihood. Running around on top of that smelly old hide pile was as second nature to me as playing on grass in the park—although obviously one was to roll around on, while the other was to run over the top of. Later, when the business took in scrap iron, running over pile after pile of protruding metal honed my skills until I was like a mountain goat in its rocky enclave. Never a broken bone, and only a few undetectable scars remain. A few tetanus shots probably helped. However, the memories of real family and personal fun with brothers, sisters, friends, and even strangers remain clear as if it were yesterday.

The warehouse that Father located and wanted belonged to George Carico. Initially, Father rented for a modest price a rather large wooden building he would eventually own. The effects of the depression were still being felt, and finding anyone to rent was hard for an owner of property, let alone a whole warehouse. Money was scarce for Father, too, but he had good credit with one of the local banks, the Twin Falls Bank and Trust, and he could get the money to operate on. Mother told Father that the family of then six children still at home could temporarily move into the top floor of the warehouse, thereby saving on the rent of a house. He didn't like the idea all that much, but she prevailed and began to prepare for the move into the warehouse as a home for her family.

The warehouse they rented had been previously used to store onions, and Mother recalls that the smell that permeated the floors and walls was very strong. Undaunted, for several days she scrubbed and scrubbed the floors upstairs and down with ammonia and soap to get rid of the smell. She doubted that the onion smell ever totally left, especially whenever any dampness from a heavy rainfall was present. I can't verify that myself, but I do remember years later the pungent smell of hides that surely masked whatever onion smell may have possibly lingered. For all the various smells and history of that warehouse, there was one particular feature that surely exemplified the ingenuity of our parents. I've told this story to lots of people who can only laugh with a certain sense of curiosity as to what kind of life we lived growing up. I've always assured them we were really quite normal, but we did have our highly unusual, if not quirky side.

I'd estimate the size of the warehouse to be 175 feet by 90 feet. The downstairs was divided into four rooms, while the upstairs was essentially one big open area, accessed by a wooden stairs in the very middle of the building. The living area upstairs was to be temporary—a few months—and so while there were a couple of interior walls, Mother felt that separating the area into various smaller sections with old bed sheets hung from the rafter was quite adequate for some privacy. Thus, everyone had a place to sleep of their own, with the boys bunked in one area, the girls in another, and our parents in a third.

Most of the downstairs space was devoted to a very large room in which the hides were stored. In the front there was an office and a second room that would sometime later be converted to a kitchen and a bedroom for our convalescing Father's needs. A separate living room would be added by our father's hands. In a small room constructed behind the kitchen was the one and only small bathroom facility with a bathtub, sink, and toilet. It was here that the little strange story of our parents' ingenuity comes into play.

To get to the upstairs, there was a set of somewhat steep stairs at the end of a long passage midway between the front office and the area where the hides were stored. The problem was that if you had to go to the bathroom from the temporary upstairs living area during the night, you had to go down the stairs, traverse the long hall way, pass through the front office, through the kitchen and finally to the bathroom. In the dark, it could take you three minutes to get there! The only other alternative was a walk down the stairs, turn right and through the area where the hides were kept and into a back door leading to the bathroom. The latter passage was perhaps fine for any adult, but what was a kid to do? Not ones to give up on a problem in search of a solution, Mother and Father decided to "fix up a rig" with a big funnel on one end of a long galvanized pipe that was stuck down through the above second floor into the toilet below. You might think of it as a downspout similar to those found to collect the rainwater at the corners of your family home. So if anybody had to go at night, they could use it at least as a urinal rather than having to trek down the stairs to the toilet. Just empty the convenient pitcher of water next to the funnel after using it, and things were fine. One of life's necessities was dealt with without as much as a thought of how it looked to others. It was a temporary solution good for a few months until more permanent arrangements were made to have bedrooms more conveniently close to the only "facilities."

In 1936, after using the warehouse for nearly two years as temporary living quarters, it had to be moved a couple blocks to a more permanent location. The necessity to move the warehouse from its original location was brought on by the fact that the owner, George Carico had an opportunity to rent the property the warehouse currently stood on to a long-term, ten-year deal with the Sinclair Oil Company. George said he would sell the warehouse to Father for a very reasonable price, and help finance it over an extended period of time, if Father would move the warehouse elsewhere. George, for his part, made the deal even sweeter by the purchase of two lots that he got at tax sale, and included these lots as part of the total purchase price. Father paid $38.70 a month over several years to buy the warehouse. Mother, ever conscious of finances and full of practicality, moved the family temporarily while the warehouse was being moved to another warehouse that was located next door to their future business location. Within weeks, both the physical move of the warehouse and the family was made without a hitch, and life went on.

The warehouse, or "The Place" as we more often affectionately referred to it, was a wooden structure of approximately 3,500 sq. feet. The Place stood on a prominent street corner along one of the major transportation routes through town, 4th Avenue West or simply "Truck Lane" as referred to by everyone in town. Truck Lane had historical significance since it was part of the old Oregon Trail on which pioneers made their way through the old Wild West. It was appropriately and informally called Truck Lane because it was the bypass route around the downtown area as mandated by the city fathers for all commercial trucks. The warehouse stood for a period of nearly 50 years, and evolved over time into simply a fascinating place. It was to become our playground, our sanctuary, the place to find our parents when we needed them, a museum of artifacts, and our parents' permanent anchor for their business operations.

The Place was gradually transformed into more suitable temporary living space over a two-year period, as well its primary function as office quarters. With the hides as part of our backyard, the Place could never become anything approaching a typical family house. Father did convert part of the downstairs into a larger office area and a separate bedroom area, a kitchen area. It had a round table where I daydreamed sitting in the very center. There was another general-purpose room that would become one day his bedroom during convalescences. He added a huge room to one side of the warehouse that became the living room, and in it he built a large fireplace constructed of the lava rock that still coats the landscape of southern Idaho, left over from a volcanic age.

In the second year at the permanent location, Mother's dad, Hazel, came to visit the daughter he rarely saw. He stayed around long enough to construct a separate, small detached house on an adjacent lot that our parents had purchased. This separate structure served as the bedroom for all three of the girls still living at home until we moved to a residence on Washington Street. It was solidly made and occupied about 700 sq. feet. During his time there with the family, Hazel often liked listening to the radio, and since the approaching war was in the news, the family often sat in the evening and heard speeches by Franklin Roosevelt, Winston Churchill, and even Adolph Hitler. The speeches of Hitler were translated by a German fellow that worked for our parents at the time. Little did they realize what impact the war that loomed would have on their lives and business. As it turned out, while the impending war would be bad for America and the world, it would provide steady income for our parents' particular kind of business. The need for scrap metal for war and industrial needs would be critical to our nation.

It was just after moving into the warehouse that Buzz was born at Mrs. Woods' nursing home, then Lorraine at the hospital, and I was delivered right in the warehouse by Dr. Drake and his wife. Dr. Drake, our family physician forever, always said that we were the healthiest kids in town. Our exposure, most likely, to every conceivable germ known to mankind because of the things stored in that warehouse, was perhaps the reason we would become immune to most things. For me personally, it's a proud mantra when I have many times explained that I was born in a warehouse in Twin Falls, Idaho. It was as good as Daniel Boone saying that he was born in a log cabin. My cabin was a pretty good-sized one and filled with all kinds of things to fire the imagination, and attract all kinds of friends. It just required looking beyond or assuming an attitude that some dirt, odors, and sights and sounds were not very important in the overall scheme of what is important in life. I suppose as a child it is far easier to overlook these kinds of things than as an adult. But I've learned as an adult that many physical and financial needs are not all that important compared to family.

After living at the site of the permanent warehouse for a couple of years, we transitioned from the Place to live across town at 189 North Washington, a couple of miles from the warehouse. The house on Washington Street was everything the normal family would want in a neighborhood of pre-1940s housing, with white-painted front porches, and tree-lined quietness. Our time there certainly had its share of fond memories, but it fortunately was our home for only about three years. The reason will be clear when you learn where we finally settled as a permanent residence.

You get the sense that our parents moved their family around a number of times during the formative days of having children and getting the business established. I never added it up exactly, but they must have rented at least a dozen homes, lived outdoors camping for what added up to about three years of summer months over twelve years, and lived an additional half a dozen years in the warehouse.

But, a time finally came when it was possible and desirable to have a permanent residence.

Just a block from the warehouse, our parents found a one-story, wood-sided house that become our permanent residence, and so we moved from the Washington street home in 1940. Our permanent home was surely in a far worse part of town, with its warehouses, a truck route through it to bypass downtown, and housing that was old, and far more rundown, and occupied by those with little economic power. It was a mixed neighborhood of mostly poor, white working class, some Hispanics, many people on welfare, and even some small businesses. There were are all kinds of lessons to be learned by living on the other side of town, not the least of which is learning how all people struggle but find joy in their own ways. But, the biggest advantage for our family was that our permanent home was merely one block from the warehouse, also located on 4th Avenue West. The warehouse would be the beacon at which our parents could be found working and it was within easy sight and walking distance—just a one-minute stroll or a 30-second run—if not shouting distance. We went between the two points as often as we wanted or needed to have their attention, or as in the case of our father, to sit at his side as he slowly passed on over after a year of convalescence. It was very comforting to us children to know that their work and our living were so close together, and it afforded opportunity to watch them at work, get answers to our physical needs, and get the emotional attention children want. Compared to today's world where working fathers and mothers commute miles and even hours between home and work, we had perfect access when and where needed. It was a perfect 7- by 24-hour-availability situation. We gladly accepted rundown surrounding of a neighborhood any day for the advantage of being near our parents.

It was the early 1940s, and as Mother often put it, "Things were going better by then." They had both their warehouse and a home. Because of the war, certain commodities were scarce. Things like tires, cars, and certain foods were almost impossible to buy. Occasionally, Mother recalled, certain items came their way and were much appreciated for their scarcity. The East Side Market came up with hard-to-get jar of Mayonnaise or Bosco, an occasional bar of chocolate, some pancake syrup and little butter for the family. On occasion, the Idaho Department Store set aside a rare pair of rayon stockings that Mother simply cherished. Or Mother's friend, Oma Whittom, the local magazine proprietor, saved a copy of *LIFE* magazine for her. For years thereafter, Mother kept those *LIFE* magazines in the upper loft of the warehouse, and I would pour over them for hours for the history they portrayed. I am sure this special treatment, for it was that, came from the close personal relationships our parents developed with others and the large family that we were. It was a sign of their establishing themselves in the community.

In their business they were beginning to handle what were called, "drought cattle" being shipped in from the Midwest from states like Nebraska and such. With the drought plaguing the land at that time, farmers and ranchers could not afford to keep their beef cattle and milk cows since there was little feed to give them. So they sold off their livestock for whatever price they could and placed them on cattle cars and in trucks to be hauled west to market. As a result, Father had the by-product of the meat market, and that meant hides.

As the Second World War came upon the nation, Father could see an opportunity that would eventually supplant the hide and fur business. He had already expanded into buying sheep pelts that were hung on long racks made from wooden poles. He hung 60 or more wooden poles in the warehouse attic where our former living quarters had been. They were two inches square and ten feet in length. Row after row hung four feet above the floor, stacked two-high with sheep pelts to dry before being sent off to woolen mills in Pendleton and Portland, Oregon. As one walked between and under the rows of pelts you couldn't help but get a little lanoline on your bare arms and hands that smoothed the skin. The smell in the attic from the drying sheep pelts was even more pungent on hot summer days when the temperature rose to an unbearable level. Of course, you might on a rare occasion also pick up a small tic, but you learned to look for these little creatures and found out how to remove them without harm to your health.

For a while, the business also took in various kinds of wild-animal furs. Trapping and fur trade were still being practiced for making women's and men's coats in an industry that would get smaller in due course. But for the time, I remember my father buying muskrats, beaver, rabbit, and fox in particular.

As young boys we learned how to go down into the Rock Creek Canyon only three blocks from our home where we would place iron traps at strategic points along the bank of the creek and catch our share of muskrats. As they would with any customer, our parents would buy the skins, and we made a little spending money for a movie or some candy.

Jack rabbits, as they are known in Idaho, are larger than usual rabbits that roamed in great abundance in the sage brush areas of southern Idaho. It was quite common in driving the highways in those days to hit two or three while simply driving from one town to another because there were so many of them. They were especially attracted to the headlights of your car, and many were killed from running out into the traffic. Local farmers sometimes organized "rabbit drives" during the peak cycle of rabbit reproduction to rid some the area of numerous rabbits that constantly devoured crops. They would run them into long nets strung across the desert, and club them by the hundreds. The rabbits quickly reproduced with as many as six litters each year, and continued to defy the attempts to rid of them. In the latter part of the 1970s, mink farmers regularly bought jack rabbits as meat for the burgeoning mink-raising industry. Mother literally bought thousands of rabbits; sometimes as many as 200 or more, they were so numerous in the area, from one individual after another. All this barely made a dent in the total population that could, it seemed, multiply faster than it could be hunted. She only purchased rabbit hides during the winter months so that they could be stored and preserved more easily in the coldness of the warehouse. They were sold as is, and processed by the mink farmer for everything from the meat to the fur.

Muskrat furs would be strung over individual wire devices that would keep the hide taut as it dried when hung from large nails on the walls serving as hangers. When ready for market, they would be removed from the wire rack, stacked, and tied into neat bundles with string. They were thrown on top of a truck loaded with salted hides and taken to Boise for shipment to tanners for processing to make coats.

By 1945 the title of the business read, "L. L. Langdon: Wool, Furs, Hides, Pelts," with a subscript of "Scrap Iron and Metals, New and Used Blacksmith Iron." Scrap iron and metals would, within a few years, become the mainstay of the business. The other commodities that had so long made up the business would be no long purchased, except for hides. These lasted well into the 1950s. The mainstay became scrap metal and mainly scrap iron. Tons and tons of scrap iron were needed for the war effort, as iron was a key ingredient in forging steel in the huge mills back East. Seizing on the opportunity, Father got into the business of buying scrap metal that came to him from every conceivable source. Old tractors, combines, wagon wheels, boilers, water heaters, plows, assorted wire, old cars, business machinery of all sorts, and on and on it went in its infinite variety. The war theme, "Every Bit of Scrap Counts," became a battle cry and a perfect marketing slogan to get people to bring scrap metal to sell. From men looking for an extra dollar to support their family to every boy and girl in town who could find a piece of scrap in the backstreet alley or their backyard to sell for enough money to buy ice cream, the scrap metal seemed to flow like a never-ending river. Even entire schools got into the fever of saving things and would call L. L. Langdon when they had a load of scrap iron or other metals.

Often as not, what was one person's scrap was another's treasure. Person after person came into the "Yard" (those other places piles of iron were stored on various lots in town) or the Place and sorted their way through the iron and other metals. The mountainous metal piles, like desert hills worn by constant wind, were ever changing, as iron was processed for eventual shipment, only to be replaced when more scrap metal was purchased. Customers sorted through the odd pieces of metal to find that special thing they were looking for to mend, construct, or fill their other needs and ideas for home or business projects. Of course, the buying price and selling price were two different things. This was, after all a business, and not some scrap heap that was your personal playground to forage upon. To our parents, buying and selling both had a fair value not to be subjected to greed for the sake of offending what would likely be a repeat customer. And, they had a special policy when it came to children, no matter the age, who might bring an item or two. Every child that brought whatever small amount of scrap metal to sell, as Mother often said, "Would certainly leave with no less than enough money—usually ten cents—to at least buy ice cream or see his or her favorite Roy Roger or Buck Jones western at the local movie theatre." For years thereafter many kids, and later, adults told me of their experience at my mother's junk yard and how much the ten cents meant to them. Many a grown man would stop our mother on the street in later years and thank her for the help she provided with their 4H project or similar venture or adventure as a kid. These and other lessons in work ethic, fair price, return on investment, customer relations, charity, respect of adults, and treatment of the very young were easier to see and understand there in the "yard" than any economics or ethics course in any university.

During the 19 years our mother and father had together, they experienced two of the most turbulent periods in American history: the Great Depression and the Second World War. All of the children between them were born or raised during those difficult years. They built their home and their business. They succeeded in their parenting, and their marriage, through sheer tenacity and hard work. Things were going well for them.

Sudden Transition to Single Mom

It was February 1, 1946 when our father, at the age of 63, died. As a young person with so much responsibility of family and business, our mother suddenly faced life's third major challenge to survival. She had lost her mother, then her grandmother, and now her husband. This challenge was even more daunting as there were six of her children, ranging from 22 to 7 years of age, still living at home. There were no insurance policies or reserve funds to fall back upon, but only her sure determination.

I was seven years old when Father died. I'll never forget that day. A friend of the family came to our school to get me, my sister, and brother, telling us we had to go home immediately. I remember walking quickly that familiar path to our home by way of the Sears building, across Main Street, and through the neighborhood I knew so well. We wondered all along why we had been taken out of school. Perhaps our old dog Blackie had died, we speculated as we walked. It was only when we entered the room where our father normally lay convalescing in the warehouse and saw our mother crying that we learned our father had passed on. After a year-long illness, he died of a heart attack brought on by lingering liver and kidney problems. I guess his smoking and drinking caught up with him. Following the day he died, our mother, herself merely 34 years of age, got up the next morning and went to work. With six children at home to support there was little time for grieving and wondering what might come next. Her husband would have expected no less of her I am sure. She remarked to a friend later in life that when she walked into the office that first day on her own, she "…felt an arm around her shoulder." She would feel that presence more than once during the remainder of her days. I take comfort that she was being watched and cared for by a spiritual being. She was suddenly at the very moment of our father's passing, the sole bread winner.

Although Mother readily understood the basics of business from the beginning, she had no plans at all for working herself. She wanted to be, more than anything, a full-time mother. Fortunately for us all, Mother had occasionally traveled with Father on business trips and had learned the fundamentals of the business. Most important was the knowledge of her husband's loyal contacts. He was a well-respected and trusted businessman who had a way with people. His friends and loyal contacts would help assure her future and ours. The business, by the time of his death, had evolved into a successful, although still fledgling, enterprise based on scrap metal and blacksmith iron. In the years ahead, she would make the business even more successful and become one of few women to own and operate her own business in our town, let alone America. In addition, she became a community leader and would establish herself as an example to all women seeking to go into business long before women's liberation became a movement in America.

The story of how she responded to adversity and achieved business and personal success is truly remarkable. It is the story of courage and the many lessons learned by her children and passed to current and future generations. In that instant of her husband's death, and through the 19 years she spent with him, followed by the 40 years when she was on her own as head of her family and business, she was the woman of iron until her own passing in 1996. What follows is the account of life's lessons we learned as her children. Through the telling of these lessons, you will come to know more about the remarkable women that we knew as our mother.

An Introduction to Lessons Learned

It wasn't until I was about 26 years of age that I fully realized how fortunate I was to have been raised by our mother. I always knew she was different and special. I think most children are late to realize the true value of parents, needing the passage of time into adulthood and the experience of parenting to realize what really happened during their life with and without us. It's then that we have the opportunity to sit down with our parents and experience them as adults who had aspirations and struggles as we do. I sat down with Mother and recorded on tape her childhood experiences, the dreams and thoughts when she was but a young person, and listened to adulthood experiences and struggles. I also took the moment to thank her again for her acts of love. At other times this took the form of writing or phoning her from afar to let her know that I appreciated her many blessings. It meant as well that things would not go unsaid that needed to be said—especially how much I loved her—because death will and does forever separate us all.

Recognition of the unique nature of my mother I hope was always there in my thoughts and actions, but it especially came to deep consciousness at the time when I was in the Peace Corps in Ethiopia from 1962 to 1964. I suppose it was the separation by distance and I had the time to truly reflect while in a primitive environment void of the noise of modern society. Curiosity pushed me to find the source and essence of such unrelenting love that she had for her children. So, I began to ask Mother about her childhood and literally anything else she could remember and was willing to share. And, there was plenty! What emerged from this inquiry helped me understand better her, the time she grew up in, and her philosophy as it applied to raising her children. The good times were plenty, and the hardships were there as well. It was particularly interesting to hear the hardships, for her view of them was so revealing of her character and approach to life. The hardships she spoke of were not so much viewed by her as lessons of grief or what didn't exist or what she didn't have. Rather, her experiences were viewed as lessons of acceptance and thankfulness upon which to build strength of character for both current and future actions in life. She met countless challenges, yet through it all she was a happy person, felt truly blessed, and was an eternal optimist. Her view of life and her experiences, I fortunately captured on a single 90-minute audio cassette tape. This material is shared with you in this book to capture the times she lived in, the struggles she faced, and the love she felt and gave to others. These experiences can be lessons of what not to complain about, and what to build on and go forth with. Also, my niece, Michelle Hiskey Smith, on her own also recorded a conversation with her grandmother, and those thoughts are reflected here as well. There were numerous articles about her business and civic activities that I have drawn upon. Her grandson, Mitchell Langdon Townley, put together a wonderful remembrance book at the time of her passing, and that has been invaluable as well. What's most personally enchanting is to still be able to listen any time I desire to the audiotapes we recorded and hear her voice again and feel the depth of her personality and love that was so much her every being. I wish for you, the reader that the words I write here had the capacity to capture what only the spoken word is truly capable of expression in inflection and root feeling. We are blessed as a family with cherished memories, combined with the many photos we have of her working, the pictures and articles of her receiving numerous awards for community and charitable causes, and the words of those many friends who knew her. They serve not only to make us feel good, but inspire us to be what she desired for us: caring and loving people.

After the nine "Lesson Learned" are described through recounting experiences that led to the lesson being learned, we will pick up and complete Mother's life story. It will then continue from the time our father died, because this is when she truly came into her own as a mature woman,   single mother, businesswoman, and community leader. The following lessons are used today and will be passed on to each generation of our families into the future.

Lessons Learned

Lesson 1:
You Are Valued as a Child

As an outcome of parenting there is no greater legacy to children than to let them know in your heart and actions that each child is valued as a person. This manifests itself not solely through the knowledge that you love them, but that you value their very being as a person in our world through your actions towards and with them. This starts by valuing them as a child every step of the way, and for what they become as a result of that love, regardless of what that may be. I believe that our mother did exactly that for each of her children in a highly personal way with the knowledge of who they were and what they might become.

I mentioned before that I spent two years in the United States Peace Corps as a teacher in Ethiopia. Having visited or worked in more than 60 countries during my lifetime, I can say that the Ethiopians do the best job of raising their children to be adults, and they do this by valuing them as children. As parents, their daily actions embody warmth and gentleness, and they permeate every act towards their children: nursing and holding them tight, smiling at them, and playfully enjoying their presence. That was the kind of feeling we always got from our mother. She never spoke harshly, never spanked, never degraded, and was always with you in her presence or thoughts. Considering that she was a single, working mother, with all the pressures attached to that, and working in a highly unusual, male-dominated profession, it is a reflection of her outstanding character that she still made her children her first priority.

Mother was always present whenever or wherever you needed her. As it was, or I am sure was planned, the house we lived in most of our childhood and Mother's "office," were just one block away from one another. The house sat at 313 4th Avenue West and the Place was situation on the corner of 160 4th Avenue West. You could literally look down and eyeball the two structures one block from one another. So, it was just a short walk to and from the house to see her or for her to come and see us. Additionally, for several years she had another "lot," which we called the "Hole" on 5th Avenue West and between Shoshone Avenue and 2nd Street West; just three short blocks from home. Actually, the Hole's location was half a square block area that was a tremendous pit from an old warehouse cellar that once was used to store potatoes. The hole was U-shaped with three walls of dirt sloping about 10 feet high, with part of the fourth end open so that a truck could drive in and out to load or unload scrap metal. The corners of the Hole had been worn from where we rode our bicycles up and down this crater year after year. At its center, the Hole was probably 20 feet deep. As can only be in the minds of children, it was as if the Hole was a prehistoric lake that had once inhabited the area and was now bone dry and filled with the remains of long lost ships. But, in this case iron carcasses of scrap iron had been deposited there on a regular basis.

The Hole, as with the "Place," as well as a vacant lot next door and one behind our house, were all filled high with varying amounts of junk (slang for scrap iron and others metals; not to be confused with garbage). The mountains of scrap iron varied in height and quantity, depending largely on how much metal had been purchased, processed, and was being prepared to make a "load"—a full railroad box car—for shipment to a steel mill. It was in one or the other of those various jungles of iron and other scrap metals that I typically found my mother, as well as my developing self-confidence as a youth and that which molded me into a healthy man. I think that how this maturation happened is one of the more important lessons to be learned, and although not exactly replicable, since most don't or can't grow up in a scrap-iron environment, nonetheless the principles are possible in whatever environment one finds oneself. It's a question of what you allow as parents and how you act towards your children when they do what they do, including their mistakes and miscues. A few stories about how Mother valued me and my siblings as children and built self-confidence through risk-taking will serve to illustrate how.

I suppose the single most important thing that demonstrates valuing us as children was her willingness to allow, indeed encourage us to explore the environment of our community in order to develop self-confidence. Self-confidence, after all, is that quality in us that frees us to explore and establish good relationships with others and our environment in order to face and advance challenges in daily living and in work to the best of our potential. If my wife knows anything about me, it is that I have a self-assured feeling of personal well-being with myself as a person. This self-assuredness drives my positive view of life, not being afraid to do things, taking responsibility, loving her and our children with caring actions, and engaging others in community. It drives me to think I can write books, rather than to keep the book inside me. I have my mother to thank for self-confidence in a number of ways, but mainly for the opportunity to explore and become what was inherently in me. I needed positive venues, and the chance to make some mistakes.

I was nearing ten years of age when two of my close friends in the neighborhood and I were in the back yard playing one bright and sunny day. The backyard in this case didn't literally mean the backyard of our house, but rather the lot that Mother owned that was directly across the alley, and upon which were the ever present-piles of scrap iron. Those huge mountains of scrap metal were in and of themselves a challenge to life and limb. We played in, on top of, and around them like most kids would on grassy lawns. But in the landscape of our environment, each scrap heap had its own peaks and valleys with objects sticking out that you had to learn to traverse or suffer the lessons of cuts and bruises that would surely follow. There were, after all, all kinds of rusting objects, such as the pointed ends of metal rods, sharp plow discs, furrows, pipes, barbed wire, wheels, gears, flat iron, sheet metal, and numerous other metal parts of once-operating machines and gadgets. We were never forbidden, but rather cautioned to be careful as we played among the iron our childhood games and made-up adventures of cowboys, knights, soldiers, cops and robbers, and dragons. Mother knew that, particularly as boys, we would have to exist in some form of harmony with that scrap iron.

Scrap iron was ever-present in our playground, and we would come to respect the dangers alongside the excitement of tinkering with the gears, wheels, rods, tires, and other objects. For example, there was an old F4U Corsair airplane that was our very own. As scrap from the Second World War, this real war airplane had folding wings, a cockpit with two bucket seats, and a joy stick that moved the flaps and rudder. We played for hours and days with it. It was, for us, a modern-day version of a battleship galactica from some distant planet. We punched and jumped on the hulk of metal until it was beaten into submission by boys and girls who replayed backyard war over and over again. We always said later in life that the Kennedys may have had a B-29 in their yard, but we had our airplane as well, and we also had things they didn't: a couple of cannons, farming combines and tractors, our own used car lot, old boilers, every conceivable tool, and nuts, bolts and nails of all metallic types. It kind of puts today's Legos to shame! I was like a gazelle on the plains of the Serengeti, leaping from one pile of junk to another. Starting with only a frame and motor (no body to cover it) I made and operated a car out of various old junk car parts. I took apart and reassembled hundreds of motors, thingamajigs, and what have you. I took my new and old friends into a jungle of adventure they simply had no personal access to on their own, and we played over and over each war game with new weapons to be found and constructed in the junk. We developed our imaginations through what we saw and what we did. If all this doesn't help in fostering self-confidence, I don't know what does. But that was just the beginning.

As I started to say, a couple of friends and I were out in the backyard. We were nine years of age at the time and we had decided to dig a hole all the way to China. Isn't that what all kids want to do when they are about that age? We didn't know that it was perhaps a long way from our position on the earth straight through to China, but we weren't concerned with geological and engineering details. Mother never said we couldn't! I remember the digging was kind of going slow for the three of us, so we looked around and came up with what was surely the solution to our slow, meager-at-best digging efforts. I am sure the person who invented huge steam shovels that carve out the sides of mountains or dredge rivers must have had the same kind of weird imagination as we boys of nine years of age did. In any case, we put together what I recall was about twenty-two old extension cords, most from our own homes, but also a few we found in the midst of the scrap iron. We strung together these various cords and led our crudely constructed trans-alley power line from the back of my mother's house, out over the back lawn, under some boards across the alley, over a couple of iron piles and into the pit we were digging to China. The pit was all of about four feet deep by now. Having the electrical supply in place—on reflection now probably diminished in power capacity by the great length it was stretched—we plugged our length of extension cords into an electrical fan we had found in the scrap iron. It was one of those old single blade units relieved of its protective wire-grill covering. In the days before air conditioning, one usually found this kind of simple metal fan sitting on a counter to cool people as they sat in their office or to cool customers as they waited to pay for merchandise in the hardware store. You can imagine that it was our intent that the fan would surely and most expeditiously slice away the dirt and rock as we dug ever deeper to China. Much to our surprise, when the blade hit the deadpan dirt with its first thrust—yes, the electrical system and the fan had worked—it landed with a thud, burned out the motor, and we were finished with that particular technological breakthrough. My mother never asked why we did it, did not comment that it was not feasible, and trusted that it was not potentially dangerous. She said, rather, that it was an interesting idea. It was like saying, "What a great notion you had. What are you going to try next?" She never said as many parents would have, "Don't try that again or I'll skin your hide." What a great lesson.

As kids, we had pretty much free access to our total immediate environment, and what a wonderful environment it was. Our immediate backyard of scrap iron would have been plenty for any child to explore, but we had access to what seemed to be the entire world, or at least our entire community and then some. Later in life, that freedom to explore was to become a platform for most of her children who have chosen to travel the world in search of knowledge and adventure. Parenthetically, it is interesting to me that we tend to do this travel not on tours, but independently, to experience not just the place we see, but the people who make it up. No matter the language barrier or the unfamiliar surroundings, or the local customs and practices, these are all new and interesting adventures to be experienced. These are opportunities to explore rather than feared obstacles to new things, people, and other opportunities. Each of us children owes our own sense of adventure to that wonderful woman who thought anything was possible and never said it wasn't.

Exploring the environment meant a wide variety of things in Twin Falls, Idaho. Unlike most sterile suburban neighborhoods of today, our community had rivers, canyons, fields, railway tracks, bridges, forests, deserts, hot springs, wild animals, livestock yards, canals, waterfalls, and on and on. We experienced this entire panoply of places and possibilities in somewhat concentric circles, as if our home were the center of the universe. Beyond home, Mother's various work places were the next point of interest and contact, and each circle beyond these two was merely another experience leading to an unlimited set of possibilities just waiting for a child to explore anywhere in the world (or universe, if only time and opportunity allowed).

Our home was a small but comfortable residence. It was a rectangle that measured no more than 28 feet by 50 feet, thus about 1,400 square feet or even a little less. It had enclosed front and back porches that were part of the total square footage. The front porch served as a place for Mother's office desk, although the real office was at the Place down the street. Also on the front porch were several indoor plants Mother liked, a large bird cage on top of a cabinet, wherein the family Bible was kept, and some old 78 rpm records. The bird was a cockatiel named Billy, and he loved to say, "Pretty Billy!" whenever you urged him to repeat his name or stoked his head. We regularly put Billy on our shoulder and walk about the house, and one day he took chance for liberty and flew out the front door. It took several hours to find him, but find him we did, about four blocks away perched on top of the old *Twin Falls Times News* building. We were able to retrieve him quite readily when we climbed the fire escape stairs to the top of the building, stuck out a finger, and he crawled on. That day looking for Billy was the day I discovered that there were more birds in the world than I had ever imaged.

The back porch to our house was a collection point for anything left over from the rest of the house, as well an extra closet and door that led to a small basement. The dirt basement was accessed by very steep, almost vertical stairs. Here canned goods could be stored, and that left barely enough space for the, at first coal and then later, oil-fired heater. Few cared to wander into the dampness, darkness, and spider-infested region that it was, but for me it was another adventure land with the added advantage of personal privacy. I took my Lionel train set down there and had great fun with friends driving the train into bars of Ivory soap. The train still exists to this day and appears annually around our Christmas tree.

In between the front and back porches were five rooms of varying size. There were three bedrooms for the five children then in the house. Mother, of course, had her own bedroom that was about ten feet by ten feet. A couple of dressers and a bed were all that was possible to fit into her room. I always remember the dresser with a mirror above it. It was under this dresser you could hear, every night upon her return from work, the thud as she dropped a money sack of change, bills and receipts for the day's work. That old Twin Falls Bank and Trust pouch is one of the items I keep in my office as a reminder of her business.

With only two other bedrooms available, there would be no space for any one of the children to have their own bedroom, let alone their own bed. My brother, until I moved in with him, was the only child that had his own room for a while. Even at that, the bedroom was more like a closet, measuring about six feet by ten feet, but it was his own room. When I moved in with him at the age of six, Mother removed the single bed and replaced it was a six-foot bunk bed that just fit the space and left us a few feet for a small dresser and a portable closet to hang our clothes. For all that it lacked in size, it had magnificent windows with small panes all along the two outside walls from about four feet up to the ceiling. At night you could open a big window that swung out and get the gentle breeze of a summer's eve and a direct view of the stars from the top of the bunk bed. Even better, the window afforded easy access to the outside, and we frequently used it to get in and out rather than use the front or rear house door.

The remaining bedroom was for my three sisters. They had the largest room. It was about ten feet by twelve feet. It had one bed, and they all slept together. Considering the needs of girls, it's a wonder they could share one room, one closet, one chest-of-drawers, and one mirror. Grateful for their new-found space, each time one of them moved out of the house to go to college, a celebration was held by those sisters who remained behind. There was one bathroom for everyone, and it measured only six feet by six feet, with a sink, bathtub, and toilet. The remaining two rooms in the house were the living room/dining room combination, and a kitchen. The living and dining room were combined in one large, grand room that occupied about 200 sq. feet. In it was a large, curved sofa, dining room table and chairs, an oil heater stove for several years, a couple of china closets, and Mother's piano organ. The grand room was a maze to get though because of the variety of collectibles displayed there among the furniture. It was the principal gathering point for eating and family activity. On the large dining room table that would seat ten, we spent hours playing cards and countless games of monopoly. The room rang with laughter, good times, and drama. The table had two leaves to easily accommodate friends and additional family for the annual Christmas and Thanksgiving events, or for when we frequently invited friends to stay for lunch or dinner. When there was not enough space at the main table, the younger kids had their own card table. Of course, who didn't want to be at the main table with the adults? Well, I guess being the baby of the family does have some disadvantage! Our sisters used to joke that sometimes there were so many kids around it was hard to tell which were part of the family and which were not.

As to the kitchen, it was small by any standard. It was at most ten feet by ten feet, and worked as a kitchen only because the refrigerator was recessed into the wall above the back stairs that led to the basement. An electric range, a sink, and two counter tops and drawers under them was all that was possible, with shelves above and in as many spaces as were left over. One single window from the far side provided the only natural light other than that which filtered in from the adjacent back porch. A small, fold-down table, chrome-lined with a plastic top, afforded the only seating in the kitchen with two matching chrome chairs with red plastic padding. It was elbow to elbow when a number of us congregated in the kitchen or came to fetch something from the refrigerator or shelves.

As a family, we ate together and took the opportunity to share wonderful moments. It wasn't unusual to have one or more of our friends stay for dinner, and it seemed they were as much a part of the family as just friends. Our sisters usually did the cooking, and any time they needed to check in with mother the telephone was close at hand. She cooked, of course, and was a master at culinary delights. Most of the family's favorite delicacies were purchased directly from the Independent Meat Company, which is where Mother also purchased large numbers of cow hides for her business. Fresh from processing, she would regularly shop at the Independent Meat Company, after picking up the load of hides, things like fresh hamburger, bacon, sausage, steaks, and the like. One of our family favorites was hot dogs, or wieners, as they were more commonly called then. These were purchased in five-pound boxes, always to be found in our refrigerator in plentiful supply. Whether lunch, or as a snack eaten raw, Mother loved those wieners, as did we all. Of course, there were lots of bologna sandwiches as well, with Pepsi, potato chips, pickles, and black or green olives. Don't get me wrong! That was lunch. Dinners were quite healthy and well-balanced. It's just that the energy we burned in play outside, without the sedentary ills of TV that capture kids today, was provided by the most convenient protein sustenance available. You might think we would have been plagued with health problems on such a diet, but to a kid we all grew up quite healthy and never the worse for it. When I think back, the only regular sedentary activity was sitting and listening to those great radio mysteries with friends and family. It kind of makes me wish TV had never come along—as much as I enjoy TV today as an adult. Perhaps television's major evil is what it does to kids who become almost completely sedentary before it, and let's not even talk about video games! Some of the neighbor kids where I live now, under the guidance of their parents, don't watch television or constantly play video games. It is interesting to watch the level of creative play these children engage in and their inquisitive exploration of the environment that they enjoy, much as I did as a kid. Makes you think, doesn't it?

That was our house and our home. It was warm, comfortable, safe, and very, very small. I almost forgot to mention the vine growing outside the front door that would often as not dwarf the entrance. It was a jungle-like canopy of foliage enticing one to find its secret entrance into the dwelling contained therein. Our house was just that—an intriguing place in its structure, contents, and surroundings and a perfect place in which to grow up. It was small, located in a very run-down neighborhood, but it was our family dwelling, and the memories of it are cherished by each of us to this very day!

As I said before, just a block away from our own front-yard was Mother's primary place of work—the Place. The Place was for us, other than our house, the next most safe, comfortable and perhaps the strangest haven in our immediate world. With the house and the Place being so conveniently located, it afforded us as children immediate access to our mother when she might be needed as she worked. "Mother is down at the Place!" became a common expression when one of the kids wanted her or when a visitor or customer inquired about her whereabouts. It was as if we believed that anyone would know what we meant by "the Place!" And the Place was to be distinguished from the "Hole," which signified the previously described depression in the earth on another lot where other scrap iron and metals were kept as the overflow to scrap at the Place. By the way, lest I let it go by without clarifying to the unknowing, the Place was sometimes otherwise called the Yard," which could also have meant the Hole. Somehow or other we always managed to know the difference—probably only by the inflection and tone of voice we communicated as children to one another. We believed that anyone else, including customers, would know what we meant. Their confusion regarding terms we used was well read on their faces, and we often had to translate directions as simply "down the street one block to your left," and/or "just across from Young's Dairy on the corner." The distinction of terminology seemed pretty elementary to us.

By the time Mother took over full operation of the business on the death of our father in 1946, the warehouse had gradually become a place that housed an array of items not found in any other business. There were, of course, the stacks of cow and horse hides that were mostly from the Independent Meat Company, although an occasional rancher or farmer would show up with that by-product of their livelihood.

The Independent Meat Company was an often-visited establishment a few miles from town where animals were processed for meat—beef, pigs, and so forth. Our parents went there at least every two weeks and sometimes more often to gather the hides that remained after slaughter of beef cattle, usually, for the purpose of producing the variety of beef products that people buy in grocery markets. As children we knew the owners very well and came to know the establishment as if it were a second home. Our fresh meat was most always purchased directly at the meat plant in large quantities. The smell of the area where the cows and pigs were processed for slaughter was one thing, while the smell where the meat was processed was another, more pleasant and fascinating place. Seeing all those pork rinds in the huge vats, bacon slabs hanging from hooks, whole and half cow sides being readied for various cuts of steaks and roasts, freshly-processed hamburger and the like was a sight not seen by many. Rather, most people saw the final products as they were sold in the grocery store and served on the table. There is an appreciation for goods and services that we learned from going to the Independent Meat Company, and other business concerns that we are allowed to go into with our mother, that is simply not experienced when you go to the supermarket and see it neatly laid out for you. We watched and learned how processing was accomplished, including the slaughtering of cows, sheep and pigs. You learned these jobs must be done by someone, including the slaughtering of animals. Through these experiences was forged an appreciation for those who do the kind of work for us that we don't see and perhaps would not do if given the choice, regardless of how unpleasant it might seem at first glance. Mother always said that, "A ditch digger is just as important as any other worker; someone needed to do it!" Believe me, seeing her do her kind of work was all the example we needed to know that a ditch digger, someone slaughtering cattle, or any arduous work deserves our appreciation for a job well done. Going to the Independent Meat Company was one of those rare opportunities to explore our environment and learn from it.

The "hides" that were purchased from the Independent Meat Company and from others, were stored in either of two locations in the warehouse on the ground level. These areas measured about 75 feet by 20 feet and were located at the back of the warehouse. As the hides were added to these areas, the "pile" would eventually reach a height of four feet. As each hide was laid out with the raw skin side facing up, a thin layer of brownish rock salt from an ever-present mountain of salt was scattered over the bare hide in a thin layer with a huge, flat shovel, much like a snow shovel but with sides. This laying out and scattering of salt was done one hide after the other as the pile grew higher and higher. When necessary, a canvas top was pulled over to keep the hides on top from getting too dry from exposure to the air. After two or three months of gathering hundreds of hides, the "pack," as it was referred to, was ready for loading and shipment to the tannery. Each hide was removed individually from the "pack" and folded by a work force of five or six men who labored under the worst of conditions—too hot in summer and too cold in winter and always accompanied by a rank smell. Working in alternating fashion, two pairs of men grab two corners of a spread-out hide. Together, they flipped the hide to clear it of the salt that had been used to cure and preserve it. They did this by pulling the hide to the end of the pack, then each man dropped one corner of the hide, and together they pulled the other corners they held over the hide itself so as to spill the rock salt that remained on the hide. They lay the hide with the fur side down, making sure not to get any excess salt on the fur. Then, together they folded the hide into a neat square and tossed its tremendous weight to the floor level in front of a waiting truck upon which it would be loaded. It required two men to toss the folded hide up and onto the flat truck bed, and that was a daunting task in and of itself. They used a kind of rocking back-and-forth motion in tandem until they felt they could heave the heavy hide up onto the truck with a grunt. Only then was the hide moved to a stacked position on "Old Irons' Side," as we referred to this truck. I saw more than one man quit under the physical strain of folding and loading hides for shipment, but never once did Mother stop. Beads of sweat would pour from her brow, but the job at hand would be done, and the men needed her management or hands-on instructions as to how to do the work, and encouragement to finish the task into nightfall if that is what it required.

When the truck was nearly full, the two iron sides and tailgate were secured. Various fox, muskrat, and other furs dried during the past few months were tied in bundles and were then tossed on top for shipment to their port of call. Finally, a heavy canvas cover was pulled over and securely lashed to the under-belly of the truck frame. The "load" was ready to be driven to the Bissinger Company in

Boise. There it would be further processed and shipped to a tannery on the East coast. Usually, my three sisters still living at home would ride along with Mother as she drove the truck to Boise. While the trip to Boise today takes only two hours from Twin Falls on the interstate highway, in those days it was a full-day's journey.

My sisters' delight in going with Mother on this venture was driven by the knowledge that in Boise there would be shopping for a new dress, opportunity to see a movie, to go out to eat at the Bamboo Gardens for Chinese noodles, and generally have a great time with their mother. Each daughter today still recalls similar trips to Brigham City, Utah, when they and mother drove to deposit a load of scrap metal (usually copper, batteries, pewter, and other mixed metals) at the Luria Brothers Company. Such trips were not without the usual side benefits that made such journeys all the more worthwhile: a taste of Snelgrove's Ice Cream, shopping at ZCMI and Penney's, and staying at the Hotel Utah. It was, as sister Bertine recollects, "…another world for us! What a thrill!"

To say the least, the smell of the hides and pelts present in the warehouse was for most people just a bit unbearable. The flies that were naturally around the Place were constant. As kids we paid far less attention to the sights and smells than did our friends. I guess it was partly having grown up in the environment that we got used to these conditions, but underneath I think it was, no matter what else, the realization that this was our parents' business and the family livelihood upon which we all depended. Our parents worked hard and honestly at achieving personal success and providing for their family; therefore, it all seemed rather natural to us no matter what the condition or smell. I've heard people say that they can't imagine what it must be like to go down and work in a sewer. Well, I can imagine! Whenever a friend remarked negatively about the conditions of the warehouse, I didn't let it bother me. I think our childhood friends actually envied our very unusual environment— no matter what the smell, looks of the place, or dirt and grime might be. It simply afforded, like no other place, the opportunity for exploration of the imagination, and a good times with our family.

One of the other vivid memories of the warehouse I have is the fly paper stickers that were hung like coils of waxy-paper from the rafters. They were designed to catch flies on the wax, and they would lie and die there by the hundreds. Later in life when I was in the Peace Corps and was again surrounded by countless flies in Ethiopia, flies were of less consequence to me than for other fellow Peace Corps Volunteers. You never know how your experiences at one time of life will come around again in another aspect of life's experiences.

Of course, the warehouse was more than hides, smells and flies. There was an office area in the front of the long rectangular building that faced 4th Avenue West. It was a corner lot, so in addition to the front office door, customers most often used the side entrance along Second Avenue where hides, iron or other things could be weighed and off-loaded or directed to other points of storage. The side entrance was an eight-foot wide door that could be slid open. Just inside was a scale for weighing loads of scrap metal or hides.

Above the sliding wooden door was a similar second floor door that could be opened to load pelts from a truck into the second floor of the warehouse where they would be hung on the long wooden racks for drying.

On the opposite wall of the front office as you entered the front door, there was for many years Father's antique gun collection. Part of my job as a boy was both to play with the guns (none of them were ever, ever loaded), and to help maintain them by cleaning and assuring their order and organization on the wall. The collection included at least 60 or 70 firearms ranging from flint-locks to blunderbusses, a fuse lock, several side arms, a Revolutionary War British musket, and even a small pistol with a knife on the end. There were also swords, knives, and even First World War and Second World War cannons that sat prominently on the corner of the warehouse lot. It was ever amazing, but a sign of the trusting times in the 1940s, that the guns were not stolen during the years they were displayed. That was until the late 50s, when someone could not help taking a nice pair of gunslinger 44s. That was the end of public display of the firearms collection—at least in the office area. The collection remains today with a grandson who values it greatly for its link to his father and his father's father.

As you entered the front door of the warehouse, to your left was one of those old railroad office, roll-top desks and a counter top with some storage area under it. On the end of the counter sat a one-drawer cash register. It was green, had a single key lock, and a handle you turned until the drawer sprung open with the ding of a bell. The cash register was seldom locked and often unattended as Mother or others dealt with customers at the back of the warehouse. If someone was going to take something in those days, it was far easier and more likely they would steal a little iron right off the lot near the alley than risk going into the cash drawer. But seldom did the business experience downright theft. When it did, the item usually ended up with the only competitive junk dealer in town and sometimes markings on batteries and such let one dealer know that the goods were stolen. But, it was truly a rare occurrence. Perhaps it was the thought that Mother was a woman in business that kept people from stealing, but I am inclined to believe it was a general reflection of the times when honesty was valued and expected by people not so far removed from the era of the depression.

On the east wall of the office was a large display case with a glass top. In it were displayed various mementoes our father had collected over the years. These included honorary war ribbons, coins, wooden tokens, rationing cards, spent bullet casings, old stamps, and the like. There was a fireplace made of lava rock collected from the Craters of the Moon site down the road on the way to Arco, Idaho. An ancient site of once volcanic eruptions, the Craters of the Moon is today a stark National Park of pure beauty and wonder to the eye. Under the two large windows that faced the street were two divans for customers to sit on, talk, and have a cup of coffee. Before his death, you could often find Father and his friends sitting there, as if it were an old country store, exchanging tales of current events and exaggerating past fishing stories over cigars.

Every one of us kids was given responsibility for something specific. For the girls, since Mother had to work to support the family, this meant taking on the lion's share of cooking and ironing. Later in life my sisters said they learned to cook by phone. Mother gave them the menu for the day and any questions they had could be answered by phone or a quick trip down the block to Mother's place of business. Mother had an on-going credit account at a local corner grocery store named the Truck Lane Market. My sisters often sent me to the store to fetch an item or two and played a game of timing me to see how quickly I could run to the store and back with the items in hand. They ordered anything that was needed, and a small receipt booklet with our family's name on it would be turned to a new page, items purchased listed, and initialed by any one of us. That was it! Every month the bill would be paid with cash money given to the girls to take to the store. Of course, many life lessons were learned by the girls in completion of these tasks, not the least of which was how to motivate their youngest brother to assist them.

For the boys in the family, there were a variety of cleanup or organization assignments. Taking out the trash, mowing the lawn, trimming or pulling weeds were our jobs. As for me, I had one special assignment that still lives vividly in my mind to this day.

From the very first moment I can remember, I was put in charge of the annual calendar display that Mother had as a give-away to customers in her business. These calendars had the business name, L. L. Langdon, on them, and proudly emblazoned the slogan: Wool, Furs, Hides, Pelts, Scrap Iron and Metals, New and Used Blacksmith Iron." Measuring 8" x 16," there were usually eight different calendars, each with a different scene depicted above the small paper monthly register at the bottom. There were the western scenes by A. Friberg of a cowboy wrangler and his lariat with a running noose in full flight as he was pursing on horseback a steer or branding a doggie. There was another calendar with a baseball scene by J. F. Kernan, or the kid and his dog at the old fishin' hole by A. Cuccmi. I particularly liked those depicting a flight of ducks or sage hens or the mother bear with her cubs at the stream by Hy Hintermeister. Annually, as the new calendars arrived in big cardboard boxes, I would carefully remove them and see how many different kinds there were. Then, I'd pound a long, headless nail to the office wall next to the office cash drawer and space the calendars equally apart in two rows and six columns. A dozen cardboard-backed calendars would fit each nail so that the customer could view and select one or more to his liking. These were the calendars for the once-in-awhile customers. Many of these calendars adorn my office today as they once did on the wall at the Place where I originally placed them so carefully and with so much pride.

For the special, repeat customers there were large three-foot by four-foot calendars rolled in cardboard tubes. These had a variety of scenes, but usually depicted a cowboy in action. He would be wrestling a steer, roping a "doggie" or riding fast-out of a desert storm that was brewing. I still have a couple dozen of these today and sometimes roll them out to once again see the historical scenes and recall the memories of place and time.

Very close friends, suppliers like the Independent Meat Company, and long term customers got the Cadillac of calendars: a hanging 12 inch by 22 inch golden, metal-lined mirror with a forest scene behind a pair of deer and a flying eagle. It also had a thermometer and the paper calendar pulled from under the mirror. It could be hung from the neatly wound cord attached to the back. Each of these relics of the past also adorns my home today and brings forth their own memories. The accountability for these calendars was a seemingly minor job perhaps at the time, but one that I looked forward to each year and loved doing. It played a small part in building my self-confidence through the knowledge that my mother trusted me to do something important for the business. The calendars were an important part of the business, and I was their proud keeper and proprietor. Mother was wise in knowing that such assignments brought self-pride and confidence to her children. Instilling responsibility and developing self-confidence through a job well done, like mine with the calendars, was certainly one of the hallmarks of our mother's growth plan for her children. One of the more remarkable examples, as well as perhaps a sign of the times, was one of jobs given to sister Bertine.

Mother regularly needed cash in her business for making change for customer transactions. So, she would write out a check once a week for $100, put it in one of those six- by ten-inch green money-bags with a zipper on one end, and would give it to Bertine to take to the Idaho Bank and Trust. This is where Mother kept her business and personal accounts. Picture a child of 10 or 12 skipping her way merrily along a four-block walk to the bank. She could barely reach the level of the teller's cage, but they knew who she was and replaced the check she presented to them with needed change in denominations of ten and five-dollar bills, silver dollars, and assorted change. The coins were rolled in paper tubes, and the bag took on a significant weight. On the way back to the warehouse Bertine would be swinging the bag around, as if some kind of toy and ever skipping like a child at play. Amazingly, no one ever bothered her. On other occasions Bertine would be sent around town paying bills in person, though these bills could have been paid by check in the mail. Mother knew that her child liked doing these unusual chores and they served as good training for various kinds of office work Bertine did in her life, including running for years the county livestock and antique fair where she lives to this day. Each child had his or her special, as well as routine, assignments to build character and to demonstrate trust. These are important lessons for any child today, although I am not certain there are many circumstances in which one would now want a child to trundle around with a sack of money. But, there are certainly other deeds of equal responsibility that can be given to children today to build responsibility and self-confidence for a job well done and appreciated.

Most likely because of the warehouse, there were all kinds of things I liked to do, and often as not took them on simply because they seemed more like fun than a chore. There was one thing located in the warehouse where a rather unusual, self-imposed chore of mine was performed. I considered it a fun thing mainly because it is just one of those things a kid would be naturally drawn to, so why not volunteer for a chore that is also fun? On the second floor of the warehouse, opposite the sliding door that led to the street below, was a large opening about eight feet by six feet, but without a door. You could step out the opening to a five-foot-by-eight-foot platform that was attached to the building and supported by two poles from the ground, and thus, the platform hung over the yard below. It was much like a wooden deck you would find outside the second floor of a house. In the center of the platform was a perfectly shaped three-foot hole. Through this hole a large eight-foot burlap bag could be hung and fastened into place by a metal ring between the bag and the rim of the hole; thus securing the bag to hang just ten inches above the floor one story below. The suspended bag was regularly stuffed with wool from the annual sheep shearing that took place every spring. The sheep had been sheared for their winter wool by local shepherds and brought to our business for sale. These bags would assure that the wool was kept dry and clean, and prepared for shipment in large quantities. The wool made its journey from the numerous sheep farmers in Twin Falls County and the surrounding area to our warehouse, and then to the wool mills. Much of the sheared wool was from a large Basque population in Idaho that free-ranged the sheep on Bureau of Land Management land over the summer, fall and winter. The BLM land was vast, semi-arid, sagebrush areas of southern Idaho. The Basque population of Idaho was the largest concentration itself of Basques outside Spain, and they had immigrated to Idaho because of the sheep farming that they had done in their old country. Father knew several sheepherders by name, having made their acquaintance over the years of fishing on the Little Wood River and several other areas of Idaho. These hardy men lived what seemed like lonely lives for months in their unique wagons in the vast regions of southern Idaho devoted to free-range sheep and cattle grazing.

Mother Loading Wool at the Railroad Siding

My self-imposed chore was to get in the bag, and adding some wool from above, stomp together the wool into empty crevices until the wool was snug in the bag, but not too tight. The fun came in stomping up and down on the wool inside an immense bag. When just enough wool was finally in the bag to be considered full, the ring holding the bag was removed and the bag was supported so that it would not fall to the floor below before being closed at the still open end. A large needle and twine was used to stitch and seal the open end of the bag. When this was completed, I remember the bag looking like it had dog ears at each corner from the stitching used to close the open end. It reminded one of huge hippos with only their ears sticking out of the water in an African stream or pond. There was a vertical ladder that was part of the platform, and you could descend it to the floor below. You then rolled the large wool bag to an adjacent storage area. The storage area looked like a large carport and was attached to the main warehouse structure. I would weigh each bag of wool on the nearby scale, label it by date and weight with a black-ink brush, making sure not to blacken the wool in the bag. The 70 to 100 bags were stacked one on another until they all formed a sloping mountain that swept from four bags at one end of the wall to one bag on the other end. When there were enough bags, they were rolled onto a truck and deposited in an enclosed railway freight car at the depot siding and sent on their journey far away to a wool mill. Of course, I wasn't the only one to perform this task, but I was part of the process, and it made me feel kind of in charge. These large bags of wool provided not only a source of income for the business, but it was a great and wondrous playground for us and our friends. Never mind the fact that one ran the risk of a tick or two climbing onto some part of your body. One need only learn, as we did, to inspect your body carefully in every crevice to see that one of these critters had not made themselves at home. If you found one, you simply learned the art of carefully removing it with a hot needle without harm to your own health, or for that matter the tick. It may seem a little gross, but there was a certain feeling of accomplishment in the experience of even removing a tick on your own. Never let it said that we youngsters were lacking for entertainment or ingenuity.

Other than the wool in the carport area, the major outside space of the warehouse was where the scrap iron was stacked, or more accurately piled. Actually, most of the piles of scrap iron were on other lots, such as the Hole, and the other locations in town. Mother usually had three or four other "lots," including the one next to our house and another behind our house. It was a never-ending process of cutting and sorting in preparation for shipment. Customers always knew, by the address for the business as 160 4th Avenue West, that someone would be at the warehouse, but not necessarily at any of the other lots. So that is where they first came with their load by truck or wagon, and even in the car trunk and backseat, to sell. When these loads were too large to be left at the warehouse, they were sent off by Mother to one of the other yards to be dumped. It always amazed me that Mother would complete a transaction at the warehouse with someone on the price of their load of scrap metal, pay them and then trust them to deposit it at some other unattended location. They were given explicit instructions on just where to "dump" their load of iron. She trusted them, and it worked! If they needed or requested help, she or one of the hired-hands would go along to help unload.

Even though in a typical day several loads would be received, it never failed to amaze me how she could recognize a load of scrap metal even after it was unloaded at one of the other lots. Maybe it had a special wheel, a twist to some metal part, or a combination of different objects or even its assorted lengths that she recognized again. I believe her visual sense of things, as well as a finely-tuned memory, were evidenced in her capacity to always know what was going on in her business. She was, after all, an astute person in many, many ways, as would be evidenced not only in her skill with business, but later as you will read in the description of her many community activities.

When a load of scrap metal arrived at the warehouse, the weight of the metal was either determined by placing the load on the scales located near the warehouse sliding side door or estimated as to its weight. The scales had a three-foot-square platform, and once the metal was positioned on it, disk-like plates to counter-balance the load would be added to the end of a balance arm. The arm itself had a small weight that could be moved along it to measure pound increments to a total 50 pounds. The total of 10, 25, 50, and 100 pound counter weights, added to the value on the balance arm, told you the total weight of the load. But, sometimes the load that was brought in was more than the 300 pound maximum that the scales could weigh. So, Mother would have to estimate the load. Rarely did anyone question the accuracy or fairness of her estimate. Or, if they did, they would haggle for a bit with her, but her word was always the final deal. She was honest to the core, and I am confident a fair and equitable settlement was always reached. More than once I satisfied my curiosity of her estimates with actual measurements on the ever-present scales. Darned if she wasn't right! It's amazing what accuracy can be developed during a lifetime of doing repetitive tasks.

If the load was a particularly big one, the customer could always be sent off to the railroad siding where the Union Pacific maintained a large truck scale for its many needs and was shared, for a price, with the general community as needed. Here your truck could be weighed both loaded and unloaded. The difference was, of course, the weight of your load of scrap iron in this instance. A weigh-slip of paper from the Union Pacific weight office brought to the Place, Yard or Hole would suffice as a "measure" or "determinate" upon which payment by check or in cash would be made. She always had at the ready her large, three-to-a-page, fold-out check registry that was used several times during a typical day. When she wrote out a check, she had beautiful handwriting, and it was all the more accentuated by her wonderful signature with a sweeping "L" for her last name. I have over the years' tried to emulate that beautiful "L," but alas, the finely-tuned handwriting gene wasn't passed on.

If the check-registry-book wasn't in the office, then it was certain to be found under the front seat of her pickup. Her business had to be mobile, and her office and all that was part of it, including the checkbook and usually a sack of money were part of that other "office," so to speak, on wheels. I can still see her going off to work with that green bank sack in which she kept the change money and weigh-slips, then returning in the evening and heaving the sack to the floor in her bedroom as it hit the floor with a thud, and slid under the dresser. By the by, Mother preferred silver dollars to paper ones. In those days silver dollars were pretty common in Idaho, and it was a hoot to make a trip to a big city, such I did to New York City one time, and see the city-slickers' eyes pop wide when you handed them a silver dollar. They were a real hit when I went to the International Boy Scout Jamboree in 1951 at the Irvine Ranch near Los Angeles and took along a roll of those dollars to trade for things with other scouts.

The remainder of the warehouse was an area next to the carport-like area. It was about 20 feet by 25 feet, and its purpose was the sorting and storing of a variety of "other" metals. There were probably twenty-five 50-gallon metal barrels at any given time, and each was to be filled with various valuable metals. If you needed it, there also was an old blacksmith's anvil with a sledge-hammer you could use to separate parts and pieces with one or more mighty swing of the arm.

You might think that scrap metal is all iron, but typically, when someone came with a load of scrap metal, it sometimes contained other kinds of metals mixed in. These could not be kept with the iron, since the mills required that the scrap iron they bought be pure, separate from other metals. Thus, the copper, aluminum, brass, pewter, cast iron, lead and other metals were separated and priced accordingly. Only tin, such as tin-cans, was not purchased, because it had little value and no use in the steel or other metal smelting processes.

Often as not those bringing a load of scrap metal didn't particularly care if it was composed of a variety of metals that brought a difference price for each metal; usually higher for those other than iron. It seemed that the task of dividing metals and the labor involved balanced one another out. So everyone was happy for the transaction as iron and the price it brought. Once in a while someone would argue the point, but they were always offered the opportunity to sit and divide the metals before sale. It soon became obvious that doing so wasn't worth the effort, and they accepted the price as originally offered. It was a lesson I learned about pricing, labor, and how people looked at things. It taught me more than a college course in economics could have. Certainly, you don't have to argue the point in the abstract, since whether you would sort the metal or the customer would was a very concrete situation and an example of contractual negotiation. She offered them the opportunity to do the work of sorting or accept her estimate, and they could judge the effort for themselves and make that clear-cut decision.

While learning many things about the scrap metal business by first-hand observation and participation would turn out to be valuable for me in later life, the underlying lesson was that I could do a variety of things and take measured risks in the process of doing so. I think that is what self-confidence really is. But, there were several other things that contributed as well, and each let me know that as a child I was valued.

One of the biggest lessons learned about being valued as a child was that you could be nearly anything you wanted to be. You had to be realistic of course. I never wanted to be a boxer, for example, but if I wanted to try I could have. But, there were certainly things I wanted to do and be. Mother made sure that if there was something we wanted to pursue that we were encouraged to do so. For example, my brother Buzz and I wanted to join the Boy Scouts. There were two different troops organized by two different churches and we each joined the one where our friends were to be found. Though it would have been far more convenient for her, we didn't have to be together, she said. We each had a great time going on numerous camp-outs where we were leaders of our patrols, earned merit badges, and led special projects and events our troop would engage in. We didn't see ourselves just as members, but often as leaders. If we wanted only to be members, that was fine as well with our mother. Participation is what was important; learning about yourself was encouraged.

Whether our mother encouraged us to go participate, or she was providing the truck to haul scouts to camp, or providing the hot dogs and soda, she was always, always prepared to be involved while working herself to make a living.

Mother was especially involved in school activities. This sprang from her own fondness of school, even though she had to drop out at the end of the tenth grade. Chief among these activities were the many class picnics where she always provided the soft drinks. For all of these many things that she supported us doing, I think the culmination came when as adults we made significant decisions in our lives and followed her example to participate in activities with our own children and our community. I believe that the way we handle many decisions today is a reflection of the way she would have handled it herself. Let me provide a brief example of when I knew my mother's example provided guidance as I made a decision regarding my own child's well-being and our future together as father and child.

I became the father of two wonderful girls in the mid-sixties. Later, I learned that one of my daughters was a lesbian. I remember well the day she came out, as they say. Even though I was surprised, without so much blinking an eye of judgment or seeking fault in myself as a parent is apt to do, my immediate reaction was simply that my daughter remained the same person that I had always known. So it mattered not that she was gay! It's exactly the way my mother would have handled the news, and indeed, when I told her she responded with strong support of my reaction and my daughter's right. Or, should I say more accurately I reacted just as my mother had in treating every person with respect, regardless of race, creed, color, or sexual orientation. Discrimination based on differences is learned in homes and in social settings, but we had a different lesson in our home. In college I walked out of a restaurant that would not serve a black student I was with. In the Peace Corps we walked out of another restaurant en mass when it was learned that it would require some our fellow volunteers to sit elsewhere. I walked in peace rallies when needed. Mother was so proud of these and other such social actions for just causes.

Accepting the reality of my daughter being gay did not end that day. Not only did I stand and provide my blessing in what I considered her marriage ceremony, even if the state did not, I spoke proudly of her uniqueness and her real caring nature for others. She is now, herself, a terrific mother of twins and provides, like her grandmother, and along with her partner financial and emotional support for her children. A few years ago when I learned that the Boy Scouts of America would no longer accept gay men as scout leaders, I returned to that organization that I so loved as a child, my Eagle Badge—the highest honor a scout can receive. I still have a picture of my mother when she stood beside me as I accepted that badge, and I know she stood beside me when I returned it in honoring my child as a human being. Thank you, Mother!

There were countless other ways in which Mother demonstrated how much she valued us, and several of these ways will be imbedded within the stories to follow as other lessons learned. I want to close this lesson learned concerning valuing our own and others' children with a particularly important reality that was always clear and dear to us children growing up.

Whenever I or my other siblings needed our mother, whether she was working or not, she was always there! Part of this was made possible because her places of work were always close at hand—within blocks. But mostly it was because I knew she was available to be interrupted, no matter what else was going on. She made that clear to me and my brothers and sisters. A couple of examples will illustrate how this commitment was manifested.

When I was bored—believe me, every kid gets bored—or didn't have something to do, I often walked down to see Mother at the Yard or in the Hole. I would usually find her with a blazing cutting torch in hand cutting iron into 3-to-4 foot pieces the size accepted by the steel mills for processing. She would be leaning over perhaps an old plow or car frame or other piece, with her left hand grasping the metal object she was preparing to cut into pieces and the right hand holding that glowing, fiery torch. She would use the torch to slice through metal like so much butter with a red-hot knife. When at last the metal was finally cut, you'd see the metal drop off and she would reach down and throw it with a flick of the wrist and forearm into an adjacent pile of already, previously-cut metal.

Mother Using Cutting Torch

Sparks of hot iron would fly in every direction during the cutting process, and in the evening dusk of a winter's day the sparks would be ever more pronounced. They would fly in all directions like one of those volcano fireworks going off on the 4th of July. The iron would drip in beads of red-glowing droplets to the ground, and as quickly assume their original color as they cooled in the dirt or melted through the white snow. Her concentration on the work at hand and the noise of the cutting, and the numerous sounds of others working the crane in the yard area could be deafening.

When I approached her there in her work with the torch, most often I'd just sit a while and take in what was going on. I could smell the flame of burnt gas as it sparked against the metal, and learned to stay just the right distance to avoid flying metal sparks touching me, lest I be burned on my skin or tiny holes burned into my pants or shirt. When she had gone on and on for what to me seemed like half an hour, but was probably only minutes, I would go over to her and touch her on the shoulder to get her attention. Deep in her own thoughts and vigilant to the task at hand, she would jump slightly from the startle I had given her. But she always immediately acknowledged my presence. She would stop her torching with a zap as the gases were extinguished, ask me how I was, what I was doing and what I wanted. And, as a somewhat-shy boy at that point in my life, I would give the classic answer of a kid, "Nothing," when in fact I was bored and wanted to do something. But coaxed to some reply or waited-out over time, I would eventually say, "I haven't got anything to do! What can I do?" Her answer was always the same and I wondered and marveled in later years at her response which was just what I needed to make me move forward and out of my sense of boredom. She would say, "Well, what do you want to do?" What a great response on her part to take the time and have the patience needed to make me decide what I was going to do. She thereby encouraged me to use my own creativity and made me feel valued and respected for having some thought of my own, if I could just articulate it to her. She was recognizing that the answer lay within my own feelings and thoughts. Not so surprisingly, I was able to come up with something that got me out of the doldrums. It wasn't a problem of boredom, but of initiative on my part.

However, I didn't go to her places of work only because I didn't know what to do. Many times as a boy I just went down to the Yard or Hole with my friends to play or just see what was going on. Of course, my friends loved the junkyard as everyone in town seemed to call it. Only we called it the "Place." And why wouldn't they like it? It was a kid's dream come true. All that scrap iron, and it's your playground! Even adults I saw years later at my 30-and 40-year high school reunions still remembered the junkyard and Mrs. Langdon. They would say, "Your mother was just the greatest," to me as if with some envy.

I remember especially well how two of my boyhood friends— two brothers with the last name of Harr, who lived just a couple of houses apart from ours at 313 4th Avenue West, would come with me, and we would stop to see my mother and say hello. We would then play in the Hole for a couple of hours before wearing ourselves out. Mother would see us sitting there, come over, and give me a quarter to buy everyone ice cream.

Next to the Hole was Young's Dairy, one of the local ice cream and dairy-processing plants. We would go into Young's Dairy and buy a quart of vanilla or tri-flavor Neapolitan ice cream. We would then take that quart of ice cream and go to the top of the onion cellar just across the road from the Hole. The onion cellar was a very large, 125 foot by 50 foot building, with a slanting metal roof made of sheet metal. The floor level of the building interior was mostly below ground level so that it stayed cool to house the potatoes or onions that were stored within the building. The roof itself was about two stories high and came slanting from its peak at about a 40 degree angle nearly to the ground, with a six-foot drop off to the street below. It was a perfect launching ramp for what we had in mind.

We would go to the peak of the roof, sit there and eat the quart of ice cream in the blazing sun—most often with our bare hands, dirty from playing in the junk. It's not like we carried spoons around with us, for heaven's sake. As much as eating the ice cream was pure enjoyment, what followed was perhaps the real goal of our mission, and it was something that could occupy us with hours of good fun. When finished with the ice cream, the wax-coated carton it came in was neatly unfolded, turned on its waxy exterior side, and used as a sled to slide repeatedly down the galvanized roof. After several slides, the surface of the roof became slicker and faster, and when you went off the end of the roof you were going what seemed to us what was at least "Mach 2" speed. I don't believe Chuck Yeager had broken the sound barrier yet, so we were pretty sure we were on our way to some kind of land speed record, although catching your pants on a protruding nail now and then could put a kid's land speed record on hold for some time. My mother from across the street surely kept an occasional eye on our frivolity during her few breaks from torching iron, and she must have delighted in promoting kid behavior that saw us exploring the environment and its small dangers with one another in real friendship. Thanks, Mom, for the ice cream!

Certainly one of the major ways our mother valued us was to let us know that we could be whatever we wanted to be in life. She had what I would characterize as a goal-centric admonishment to us that was repeated many times and in many ways. She never once told us what to be, but only that you could be whatever you wanted to be. She once was quoted in a local newspaper article, "It's hard to tell anyone how I raised my kids. Each one seemed to help the next one; I can honestly say that not one of them ever gave me any trouble." That is a lot of credit given to us, when the reality was that her love and belief in us made us want to please and to be what she wanted so much for us—to be what you are in side you. To quote again her words in that article: "A child reminds me of a flower—it's the way they seem to unfold from birth."

Before our father died, he set up his oldest son, Lynn, in his own scrap metal business in a nearby town. In later years as Lynn was truly on his own, he developed a highly successful business in structural steel and fabrication of farm-related storage bins, irrigation pipe, and other farm-related needs. Our brother Archie, after a brief career in trucking, went into business with brother Lynn.

The remaining six of us also went on to be what we decided to be, just as our mother had encouraged. Sister Dorothy always wanted to be a cowgirl; she met and married a genuine cowboy rancher, raised two fine daughters, and lived her dream of raising quality horses and living in the country, as she does to this day. Plenty of childhood dreams were played out on our older sister's ranch by her brothers and sisters.

The rest of us had a yearning for college, and Mother, even though she only finished the tenth grade herself, was a strong advocate of higher education. Sister Lucille went to UCLA, studied drama, and became an accomplished dance teacher. She choreographed and directed many amateur, but professional-looking productions over a 40-plus-year career, while raising three children of her own. Sister Bertine also went to college before taking on her life's desire to do secretarial work. She married and settled into dairy-farming with her husband, which she dearly loved. Like her mother, she, too, lost her husband at a young age, and also like Mother got up the next day and provided a living for her four children, all of whom subsequently excelled at college and in the business world. Again, like Mother, she was honored as a parent by being named an Idaho Merit Mother, and on many occasions in her community, honored as a Distinguished Citizen. Her four children had the great distinction among the grandchildren of knowing their grandmother first-hand as she lived on the farm with them during her retirement days. They came to know to a large degree what we as children experienced, as I am trying to relate here in story and description. If you ask any one of Bertine's children about knowing their grandmother, they will shine with great love and affection from having known her personally, as will the others in our extended family. What a legacy to live with and reflect upon!

Brother Buzz loved theater, much like our father, and worked in the field of journalism. He was the General Manager of a TV station for many years, Editor-in-Chief of a five-newspaper enterprise, and head of the Chamber of Commerce in Twin Falls before his untimely death from cancer at the age of 53. The plaque commemorating his contribution to the community may still be found at the visitor's center that bears his name. The Buzz Langdon Visitor Center is located on the south side of the Snake River canyon as you cross the Perine Bridge at the grand entrance to Twin Falls. His service to his community was a lesson learned from his mother's own service to that same community.

Sister Lorraine, ever the lover of religious things as Mother would later say, married a childhood sweetheart and went off to serve others through a campus ministry program. Later she lived out her Christian life in constant service to others. At present she and her husband are part of saving The Lost Boys from the Sudan. Again, she is following her mother's service to others.

Finally, I wanted to be and became a teacher and practiced my profession for three years here in the US and abroad as a Peace Corps Volunteer. My heart took me to the field of training in corporate America, and I presently enjoy a successful consulting business with my wife and partner in life and business. I have developed a model of work that has contributed to business understanding and solution of organizational needs. As an author and business "model maker" I am doing what I love and know that my mother made possible for me. I am and remain her "baby boy," and it's a mantle I wear with great pride.

Each of Mother's children has achieved professional status as their talents and desires led them. They have created in their personal lives as husbands and wives and parents, the kind of desired normalcy that produces contributing members of society. Each has his or her own life's problems that they are quite able to cope with and resolve, in measure because of how they were reared to deal with challenges. Thank you, Mother, for encouraging, supporting, and valuing us to be what you knew we were capable of being for ourselves and for others. Those lessons in learning to play a musical instrument, which we all did, in camping out in the backyard and in nature and surviving, and letting me cook a hamburger on an open fire in the backyard with my friends, and other character-building experiences really paid off. I felt valued as a child, valued now as an adult, and I am able to meet life's challenges with assured confidence. Thank you, Mother, for the lessons learned about valuing yourself. Thanks for the lesson in valuing children.

It is important to say that she not only valued us as her children, but she equally valued every child. If it wasn't making sure every child who entered her business left with a minimum of ten cents to buy ice cream, it was her contribution to the many Future Farmers of America, or numerous other youth groups who might need some free metal part to build their projects for the county fair. Our house was like a zoo of kids, in and out, staying for lunch or dinner, or staying overnight and hanging out with a brother or a sister. It was a hideaway, a playground, a safe haven and a refuge, in addition to being a place to get emotional sustenance or a hot dog to eat. Our home was a community, and our community was our home. Our mother was the provider and mentor for that community.

Lesson 2:
Learn from the Lessons of Life

When my wife hears me tell stories of growing up, she wonders how I ever survived long enough for her to find and marry me. She is right to some degree, in that I did a few life-threatening things. For me, the time, environment, and experiences were all normal and natural. That's because our mother never discouraged taking risks, because that's the way you become confident in what you can and cannot do. I think she knew the risk, but the risk was worth the growth in positive lessons learned that would be used throughout our life. I know there were certainly things I did that when revealed to her in later life made her gasp or exclaim, "You kids!" But, for the most part, that freedom to explore and challenge our living environment was all part of what she allowed and encouraged so that we would learn, broaden our horizons and become better for the experience.

In case I wasn't clear enough in describing our house and the business, let me say that we were definitely on "the other side of the tracks," as people like to say about those who live in the more depressed area of a town or city. Ours was the area where the big semi trucks and lots of through traffic traveled to avoid the center of the town. It was the West side, and bordered the South side which wasn't much better. We were on the side of town where the canyon of Rock Creek flowed, and the Union Pacific Railroad chugged through our town just three blocks behind our own back yard. This was also where the train-bridge, the creamery for making butter and cheese, the flour mill, several furniture-storage warehouses, and bean and potato storage cellars were found. Stew Morrison's tire business, Ernie's Blacksmith Shop, the Idaho Feed and Seed Company, the International Harvester dealer, the ice-making company, the locksmith, and Young's Dairy were just some of the businesses. There also was our parents' business.

The neighborhood was mostly rundown, vintage-World-War-II-or-older housing. Residents didn't especially, with some exception, take care of cutting the grass or hoeing the weeds often enough. You could occasionally hear fighting between angry parents or see the hobos and tramps near the train trestle. Living just across the street from the Studebaker car dealer, with new Edsels, made you wonder how well business was going. A personal favorite was the Conoco gas station on the corner, between the house and the Place, where I could get free maps of different states and wonder what it was like in other parts of America. Another favorite was the Pepsi bottling dealer where you could peek in the window and see all those wonderful sodas making their way along the conveyor belt and the caps so neatly attached to the top by a machine. I always wanted to work there one day, but never did. Instead, I worked a couple of summers at the local ice creaming factory, and that was even better.

Our mother, although we never asked her, could probably have afforded a better neighborhood for her family. She surely chose the location she did for a far more important reason. Her children would be near her should there be any need on their part, and she would have the security of knowing we were close at any moment—especially since our father was no longer around. Frankly, it wasn't until we all got to high school that any one of us among the kids made anything of the difference between us and the others in town. Somehow or another there was a perception that you were better off if you attended the Washington or Bickel elementary schools as compared to Lincoln Elementary on our side of town. We loved Lincoln Elementary and our neighborhood. Actually, we had many friends from across town who desired our freedom, the obvious fun we were having with each other, and access to a wonderful junkyard. Up until our friends reached the teen years, what they really wanted was to live where we did—and live how we lived. Of course, we had to explain the smell of the Place and the junk yard mess on the lot next to the house, but there was nothing about the environment that others didn't desire in their own way. It was, after all, relatively safe and full of so many things to do.

The neighborhood, by most standards might be considered rough and tough, and we learned to respect the environment we found ourselves in. There were no gangs in those days, so we didn't have that to contend with. Through the years we got to know and use our neighborhood as growth experiences, rather than self-destruction as can happen now, such as with graffiti and gangs. I believe, for us, to respect our environment started during the early days of camping on the Little Wood River for the summer. There you fished and took only what was needed, and you left the wonderful forest and stream the same as the day you first found it. We treated our neighborhood the same way.

Just three blocks south of our house was the Rock Creek Canyon. As canyons go, it's a relatively shallow one, 80 to 100 feet deep on average, and 250 feet at its widest point. The canyon runs the length of the southern part of town from beyond the stockyards to the northwest end at the hospital and beyond—at least that's the part of the canyon I roamed throughout my childhood. Depending upon where you decided to descend into the canyon, you could either climb some of the rock walls, or find a path through the rocks to take you down to the meadow and creek below. The creek averaged 15 feet in width and meandered with the canyon walls it had created, and it was blanketed with grassy areas on both side of the creek banks. There you could fish, or as we did for a while, trap muskrats and sell the hides to my mother. We duck-hunted during the winter, fished in the summer, explored the water-filled tunnel that came out of the canyon wall at one point. We crawled or walked the big pipe that crossed the creek at another spot. We hunted on the canyon walls above for numerous small lizards that could be found sunning themselves on the rocks. If you really wanted to be adventurous, you learned to traverse the wooden train track, keeping an eye out for a freight train should it happen to cross when you did. Those with true grit walked the train bridge, not on the top with its wooden catwalk next to the track, but underneath the bridge on its support struts and wooden cross members, rich with the pungent odor of creosote preservative. Here too, you would occasionally meet a tramp or hobo as he worked his way through town by hitching an illegal ride on railroad box cars and their engines that frequently came through and over the train bridge. Mother knew we played there and other similar places, and she relied on the belief that we respected the environment and the dangers it held. We learned from experience how to press our luck only so far. Most of that luck was forged in playing in the junk yard with all its perils. It prepared us to carefully scale a canyon wall, walk steadily through waters with swift rapids, and traverse whatever the environment threw at us. With some scratches and scrapes, we survived many a scare and learned respect for the environment based on its hazards as well as its many potential payoffs. Later, as an adult, I realized that taking such risks early in life prepares one to take calculated, and I emphasize the word "calculated," yet realistic risks later in life. Life is for living, including traveling the world, and if I had not learned skills in risk-taking, I doubt I would have traveled the world as I have done, met the challenges of work, marriage, and even divorce. Thanks, Mother, for letting me explore that canyon and far beyond its borders.

There was one place in particular that was a favorite part of the Rock Creek Canyon. It was a place that each of us children experienced in common and to varying degrees. Just west from the present hospital in Twin Falls was a small farm on the rim of Rock Creek known as the Prescott Farm. You could easily walk the two miles to it either through the windy canyon or across town by navigating the back streets and alleys you knew so well. The farm was mostly comprised of a corral area with a white, wooden fence encompassing a large riding area for Shetland ponies—those small horse-like creatures with their own particular temperament. We would often go there to occupy the day and play cowboys on a pony. That could take up lots of time. It cost 25 cents an hour and was a real treat. If you weren't riding yourself, you sat on the fence and encouraged the antics of others riding. Often as not we would meet kids from town who were easily convinced to come home with us to play in the iron pile by the hour. The Prescott farm represented for us children one of the many safe havens in our town where we could play, meet others, and extend our realm of experiences. As with the various Langdon scrap iron locations, kids in those days had places to go and be free to be kids. It was safe, fun, and it made childhood all that it should be.

Of course I did do some really stupid things also. When I did, I usually owned up to them with my mother because I respected and did not want to disappoint her. For example, I'll never forget the time when I was about 15 years old, when I and a friend of mine, Mac Soden, decided to try something we had only heard about from others. It involved standing on opposite sides of a quiet neighborhood street and pretending we had a rope between us even though we really didn't have a rope. As a car would pull close and see the two of us standing on opposite sides of the street, we would act as if we were pulling on an imaginary rope to make it taut across the street. The startled motorist would come to a screeching stop. Of course we had a big laugh, took their verbal abuse or simply ran over to another street to repeat this foolish behavior. At the end of a day of perfecting this trick, we were over on 2nd Avenue North, near the Catholic School and when a car approached, we flanked the road and pulled on that imaginary rope. Sure enough the car came to a stop, but this time one of two men in the unmarked police car rolled down his window and said, "Langdon, if you don't stop that, I am going to tell your mother!" It was an off-duty policeman she knew. I immediately repented and never did that again! "Thanks, Mother, for being known in town. No, really; thanks!"

Then there was the time when I was about nine years old, and an event occurred that my mother didn't learn about until about forty years later. I tell it only because afterwards, I vowed not to risk doing anything similar in the future that would surely have embarrassed my mother had she learned at the time about this particular incident. She always said, "I don't care what you do, but don't do anything that would bring shame to me or our family in this community." It was a proclamation that defined limits on our behavior, and though I am sure most of the others things I did would be considered mild pranks or just childish behaviors, this one was more serious, considering what could have happened.

The Harr brothers and their cousin and I were kids who did the usual things in the neighborhood. We played corner games of kick-the-can, listened to the Green Hornet on the radio, played cowboys and soldiers, played some little league baseball and a neighborhood game we called "Anti-I-Over" that we played hour after hour until the sun went down. We also had a club for boys only, and naturally a variety of club houses. One of the club houses was in an abandoned house cellar. It was located across the alley and three doors down the block, across from the Harr residence. A cellar house has no upper floors to it, rather every living space is below ground level, and the flat roof is only two or three feet above ground level, so that a few windows can cast light into the otherwise dark domain. It had long been abandoned, and the roof was now missing, so that all that appeared were the empty rooms below. In one of these rooms was our clubhouse. That's where one of the guys dared a neighborhood girl to show her young breasts, which she fleetingly did for about two seconds. So much for early sex education! We also had a club house in the upper stairs of Mother's warehouse. It was kind of cool because it was plastered on all the walls with paper Pepsi Cola bottle labels we found one day abandoned in an alley. It was the year the local Pepsi bottler converted from the then-paper labels to embossed labels on the glass bottles. Often as not, the smell of the hides in the warehouse prevented us from meeting in that clubhouse for very long.

Our favorite clubhouse—the one for boys only—was situated next to the local Coca-Cola warehouse a few blocks away from home. It's where the soft drink company in question stored the old wooden crates that held 24 bottles of coke. These were the empty cases, and it seemed to us that there must have been a million. Besides playing on the stacks of cases and moving them around to configure any kind of fort we wanted, we made a secret passage from the very top of those crates, down into the bowels at ground level where we had a 4 x 5 foot area for secret meetings. One fine sunny day we were on our way to this clubhouse, and on our journey we happened by the local dry cleaning establishment near the Park Hotel, a couple of blocks north of the warehouse. We had an interest in the dry cleaning establishment only because in the back of it, near the alley was a pile of a grey, dusty, dirt-like substance. We had, on previous occasions, discovered that when a match was applied to this substance it would burn with a soft, but not highly visible flame. Thus, we called it "Burning Dirt!" No doubt it was some kind of hazardous material from the dry-cleaning process. On reflection, we should not have been playing with it any more than the liquid Mercury we found in old heating thermometers in the junkyard, but then we didn't know the difference. In any case, after collecting some of the Burning Dirt we made our way to the club house with the dirt in a paper bag, along with candy bars and popsicles to idle away some of the day. Neatly situated in the club house at the bottom of the Coca-Cola crates, we lit the dirt, and stayed for a while doing some mumbo-jumbo over the lit flame from which you could barely feel heat. As we closed off our meeting, I can still remember to this day—as clearly as it was yesterday—that upon our climbing out of that hole I asked one of the guys, "Did you make sure you put the Burning Dirt out?" "Yes," was the reply from someone. Well, we were just about two blocks away, near the old horse corral where my sister

Dorothy once had boarded her favorite horse, when I turned around and looked back to see that stack of Coke crates smoldering in white smoke from a small fire. About that time, we heard some fire engine sirens, and we took off in the opposite direction from the Coca-Cola warehouse and its soon-to-be, we believed, flaming inferno. We walked quickly in what can only be described as that odd way you see someone power-walking with highly accentuated swinging arms and giant, broad steps. On reflection, I know it must have looked rather odd to most people to see four boys going away from a fire, while everyone else was going towards the looming smoke. I never told Mother about that experience when I was a kid, but it surely weighed upon my conscience until I was nearing 50 years old, and I confessed to her. In there was a lesson about knowing right from wrong, and it would have been better to have told my mother much earlier than not. By the way, the fire was quickly extinguished by the fire department and did not cause extensive damage, except perhaps to our sensibility. It was a lesson learned the hard way.

Later, when I was 16 years old, there was another incident of a different kind, but similar in scope. For this I voluntarily surrendered my driver's license because I had done something wrong. Perhaps the experience at the Coca Cola warehouse had taught me a lesson in conscience building. I knew my mother would have said that surrendering my driving license of my own accord was the right thing to do. Still it was hard to do, but I did it, and was forever grateful for having learned to take responsibility for any of my stupid actions and mistakes. That meant losing a friend or two along the way. For example, when my best friend stole some caps for his cap gun from the Woolworth store in town, I knew I could no longer consider him a friend, and I ended that friendship one evening on his doorstep knowing it was the kind of thing my mother would say was needed. It was better to give up things because I wanted to, rather than having my mother tell me I had to. Thanks, Mother, for the lessons in learning right from wrong. If I had only learned such a lesson at the tender age of seven when I nearly cut off my thumb using the butcher knife to cut the tongue off a pair of old shoes to make the rock holder for my beanie-flipper (known perhaps better to you by the name slingshot)! I should never have used that old butcher knife that was used to cut the ears off hides that were to be salted. I would have avoided the scar that resides upon my index finger to this day. It's easier to repair the scars on your conscience when you know the person you love most will forgive and make sure you learned from the experience. Thanks for tolerating the scars and promoting the healing process of so many childhood experiences, both bad and good.

Lesson 3:
Respect Your Parents and Yourself

Since our father died when I was seven, I didn't have him around to teach me the uniquely boy or man things, but I can say in all honesty in my case it didn't really make a difference. This was because our mother was both a feminine and masculine figure to me. I think it helped me appreciate both sexes in ways that separate roles cannot. Besides, I had older brothers who filled the man-gap quite nicely. We certainly knew from our mother that you should have respect for your parents, and in so doing that you show respect for yourself. The interesting lesson for me was that respect of parents doesn't come about because of what they say, but rather it comes from what they do that makes you respect them. In turn, you understand how to show respect for yourself through mirroring that parental character through actions of your own.

I don't think my mother believed that everyone deserved to be liked. She'd sometimes remark that this person or that one was just, "An ornery sort!" She didn't know what made him or her so, but it wasn't your responsibility to fix him either. You should be nice to them up to a point, and tolerance was the guiding light for your own actions. If you choose to act in any way like them, you might just end up being one of them yourself.

My guiding light for practicing respect for others came from viewing my mother as both a mother and father, or if you will, a feminine and masculine role model. The following description of our mother guided my response to numerous events and circumstances in my life.

I used to see my mother go off to work most everyday just about the time I was getting up to have breakfast and go off to school. I would usually first see her around 7:00 a.m. dressed in Levi jeans, cowboy boots, a long-sleeved flannel shirt, a red-and-white or blue-and-white bandana wrapped around her hair to the back, her business checkbook under her left arm, and that money bank deposit bag held tightly in her right hand. This daily ritual of preparation for work was like clockwork. In winter it meant being up and at work before the sun came up. She needed that form of dress because she would be spending the day cutting iron with a torch, dealing with and paying largely male customers, loading iron, and directing a crew of three or four men. The days were long, most often 12 hours. Her appearance when work was finished and she walked in the door, usually around six or seven p.m., was quite different from that of her morning departure.

In the evening you would see entering the front door the same Levi/boots/shirt/bandana combination as had left that morning, but now she was generally black as coal from the dirt and grime of being in the iron pile. This would be even more accentuated during the summer months when the hot temperature reached that point where sweat and brawn were magnified by a long-day's work. For much of the work day she wore a pair of green-shaded, round goggles to protect her eyes from flying metal sparks while using the cutting torch. On removal of the goggles, which had been surrounded by the grime on her face, one saw two perfect circles within which was her white skin and bright blue eyes. To the unknowing it could have been spooky, but to the knowing it was those beautiful, smiling and loving eyes peering out from the mask of a hard day's work.

Her first act, after putting the checkbook down and slinging the money bag under the dresser in her bedroom, was to greet everyone, ask how the day went, and then go off to the bathroom for a quick bath. What followed was a daily transformation never to be forgotten and startling, on the order of being crowned "Queen for a Day." Out of the bathroom, after about 20 or 30 minutes, would emerge a woman now wearing a dress, make-up, and lipstick—as perfect a figure of womanhood as possible. It was a transformation from the masculine to the feminine figure. Sometimes, the transformation was needed in order to go out after dinner to lead some volunteer group at the church or other community organization. Sometimes, it was to rest her weary bones for the evening as she puttered among the roses she loved to tend, or read a copy of *Sunset* or *Life* magazine. Whatever the purpose, the contrast of your mother going and returning from work, in some sense as a man doing "man's work" and then seeing her emerge from the bath transformed as a woman, was a powerful image. Whatever images you personally have of your parents, and of course we all do, the one clearly burned in our memories was the sight of our mother transformed daily from the hands-on worker and business person that she was to the woman that she also was. It's no wonder in our family that you grew up never thinking of discriminating against anyone based on stereotypes; certainly not against women, nor anyone else, for that matter, based on gender, faith, creed, sexual orientation, or life's economic circumstances or choice. To do so would be an affront to the example of our mother, and more, the actions and being of that fine person whom we were lucky enough to have as a mother. Respect for her came easy, and therefore respect for others who were deserving was an extension of a lesson well learned and never forgotten.

There were other ways in which respect was learned. I used to love to go to the warehouse and to the yard whenever possible. Perhaps as the last of nine children I needed that contact more since the older we all got, the more of us were out of the house and on our own. As a result of my many trips to her places of work, I had the opportunity to see my mother in many interactions with customers, mostly men. Her skill with customer relations taught several lessons that I use today. My wife says that I am able to get virtually anything from anyone. In this world of impersonal human interactions, a little kindness, a smile, and recognition of others' work goes a long way in getting what you want and need. You'd be surprised how many times I've been upgraded on an airplane or had a late interest penalty forgiven, or what have you, simply because I was courteous to those so rushed and hassled by the usual customer.

It was fascinating to watch grown men who must have thought of themselves as strong, independent souls dealing not with another man, but a women in a "man's world." Many were hard-nosed ranchers and farmers. Others were independent owners of businesses. There were also migrants and hobos who collected scrap in the alleys and along the roadside to sell. Most were pretty nice, but some were just cantankerous! What was there to argue about? Scrap iron, pelts, wool, furs, or whatever were tangible items. Each item had a value according to its weight and sometimes its quality. These men could witness, if they chose, the items they brought for sale or purchase being weighed on a balance scale. They might argue that the price was too low when selling at the time because a month ago it was higher, but these were market-driven prices dictated by the mills and tanneries. They might argue that the weight she estimated for a load over the maximum three hundred pounds the scales could weigh was inaccurate. But, they were more than welcome to go to the scales at the Union Pacific railroad and pay the fee. Or, there was another scrap dealer in town they were always welcome to go to and were directed to its exact location. In general, the business of buying and selling scrap metal and other commodities that were Mother's business was a mutually beneficial and satisfactory transaction. They had something to sell, perhaps for some extra cash beyond their regular jobs, and Mother was in the business of buying what they brought in. But, now and then, there are just some cranky people.

Sometimes the crankiness came from those who just tried to defraud you. They might add some water to the sheep pelt so that it weighed a little more. They might place some heavily weighted item in a large load weighed at the railway depot, but not include it when brought to the yard to be unloaded. They might argue the issue of how much copper, pewter, brass, lead, or other metal was mixed with iron at its lower price. They usually failed to consider how much extra time it took to sort each metal out or to cut the longer pieces of iron into a suitable size for shipping. Whatever the disagreement, or lack of understanding about processing metals, they would argue their point of view. My mother's response was standard. It was a kind of quiet, "Well, I can see your point of view, but the facts are…" way of looking at and explaining things. She would not raise her voice, but she would keenly look each one in the eye, cock her head slightly to the side, and explain her point of view in a matter-of-fact, even tone. It was only when they choose to use a misguided curse word, or perhaps mistakenly challenged her integrity, that you would see her demeanor change ever so slightly. She became precise and spoke frankly. You were always welcome to go elsewhere with your business and she would give you directions to that other dealer's location. "Well, you can always check with Luke Francis, the other scrap dealer for a better deal!" Sometimes they would, but often they returned later with head hanging just a bit lower.

On the rare occasion I saw her get really mad at some customer, she knew he was just trying to be a cheat who seemed to believe that he could bully this woman into submission. In those really rare instances, she flatly told them to get out of the yard and not to return. She didn't need the aggravation, as she used to say. Life just wasn't worth the anger, and beside there were just some "…ornery people in this world, you know." Thanks, Mother, for giving me this lesson in patience, but also for standing up for my self in what I know is right.

Sometimes what my mother didn't say also demonstrated a fundamental respect for others. Mother was not much of a social conversationalist, although she really could have any discussion on virtually any topic and hold her own. I think there was much in what she didn't say, as well as what she did say. My wife has often commented, as have others, that I don't say a lot (as was the case with my mother), but when I do it is usually either somewhat profound or pretty funny. Later we'll get to the importance of humor in our family. I think Mother's patience was something I acquired from watching her deal with business situations that called for patience and fairness.

There was one particular time (other than being part of setting that accidental fire at the Coke warehouse) when I did something rather stupid. I was about 17 years old, and three of my friends and I were dragging Main Street, as was often the case with teenagers in those days. We were cruising from one side of town to the other. The town was so small that you could easily traverse it in about 10 minutes going the legal speed of 25 miles per hour. At one end of Main Street on the east side and out on to Filer Avenue on the west side were two drive-ins that had the best hamburgers and milk shakes in town. Well, one evening when we were pretty much minding our own business, a load of guys in a hotrod from another town came up beside us and began ragging on us about something. I, for one, knew that trying to out do character assassination and bravado was not a smart thing. However, that wasn't true of one of the other guys riding shotgun in my car—last time he rode with me—as he yelled out a few less than wonderful remarks, and then proceeded to spit on the other car. What resulted was an advanced version of teenage road rage. Pressed to somehow or another extricate us from what I perceived as personal danger, I wasn't very smart in trying to elude them. They sped close to the back bumper of my car over several blocks, chasing us to prove they were tougher, which they definitely appeared to be. As it turned out, I knew the town better than they did and made my way to an old car garage within which we could hide undetected. Thus, we made our way out of that jam. Of course, getting out of one jam and getting yourself immediately into another can be a sign of the unknowing. The problem was that the garage in question, an abandoned Studebaker display room, was a garage that Mother had access to store her work and personal vehicles. It was directly across the street from our residence. Mother, working late on updating her business books in her office on the front porch to the house, saw our narrow escape into the garage from a pursuing vehicle. When she confronted me with my dubious behavior with the car—the next day, rather than that evening—it wasn't what she said to me, so much as that I knew I had to tell the truth. It was respect for her that led me to suggest a self-imposed suspension of my driver's license for 90 days. Not, mind you, directly with her but rather with the local sheriff's office. Thanks, Mother, for letting me learn to confess my bad deeds and mete out some self-imposed and appropriate at-home jail time. That 90 days, by the way, turned into 180 days when the sheriff so unkindly lost my driver's license in his desk drawer. One bad deed can sometimes be compounded due to uncontrollable circumstances.

There was one other aspect of garnering respect that I think is especially worth noting about Mother. Mother had a favorite spot to go for lunch practically every day of her working life, as well as on many occasions for dinner, as more and more of her children left her house to be on their own. Most of the dining out occurred when I was 12 to 18 years of age. By that time, most of my brothers and sisters were out of the home, and Mother preferred eating out to fixing dinner. She was a great cook, and I knew how to cook myself, but as she got older, I think her energy was taken up at work, and she enjoyed relaxing with one or two of my sisters and my brother and me at her favorite local dining haunt. There she also found loads and loads of personal and business friends. The Depot Grill, as it is still known, was practically a second home to us. We knew the owners, who were also the chief cooks and bottle washers, like they were relatives. In the days, months, and years of dining there, we were such good customers that if there wasn't room in the public seating area of the Grill for us, they often simply created a table in the kitchen and we ate there. Not exactly what you can get away with today, but it was a small community, and we knew one another very well.

The Depot Grill, to this day, is classic Americana. It is situated on a major street corner that marked the way out of town on the south side, just before the singing bridge. The bridge was called the singing bridge because it had metal corrugates of steel that would hum as rubber tires passed over them. Thus, it sang to you as you drove over it.

Depot Grill

As you might guess, it is called the Depot Grill because it is located within a couple of blocks from the site of the old depot to the Union Pacific Railroad. The main railroad tracks used to run through Twin Falls at this point. Freight of all kinds, including cattle, horses, as well as the scrap iron of Mother's business, was railed through a large switching yard. Just a couple of miles away there was a big roundhouse where you could see the engineer turn the train engine around on a huge Lazy Susan-type contraption. Can you feel the excitement of the variety of things this town offered?

In the days we dined there, the Depot Grill had a long counter that wrapped 90 degrees around one end, with a row of swivel-seats. When you entered the front door, you were about in the middle of the counter space where the cash register sat. Across from the counters, next to the windows were booths that could easily seat four to six patrons. When I was growing up, at one end, out in the open, were a wash sink and a towel that hung from a hook. The grill was frequented by regulars, most working people, and they needed a place to clean-up before a meal, and thus, the sink right out in the open. At lunch time especially, people would typically enter and have to wait for a while because of the busy lunch traffic. Besides the regulars, there were farmers, those who worked at the local ice factory, grain millers, truckers, or simply those who found their way there as travelers who had asked a local where the best place in town was to eat.

As I said, because we ate there so often, the Depot Grill was like a second home to me. I even remember taking a few dates there to eat dinner before a big high school dance. What constantly amazed me, besides the great fried chicken, coconut cream pie, and beef and shrimp was just how many people my mother knew. We would walk into the grill, usually make our way down the left side to our favorite booth if available, and along the way there would typically be somewhere between six and a dozen people who would either stop her and ask how things were going, or acknowledge with some greeting or a simple nod of the head. They might want to know simply how business was going. Or, they had seen her picture in the paper, and would congratulate her on some community activity she had done recently. They would know one of her children and inquire how she or he was doing at college or perhaps they would comment on the dance recital that they had seen the night before, orchestrated by her daughter, Lucille. Or, it might have been Bertine winning a state bowling tournament, Buzz's part in a play or his singing with his jug band at the high school, or some other accomplishment of one of her children. Maybe they were from a ranch or farm miles away and were just in town for the first time in months, and they wanted to recollect the time she and our father had come by and stayed the night. Or, there was a thank you for letting them have the hospital bed she had lent them to use for their ailing or dying loved one. She was like a radio beacon to which signals of gratitude, congratulations, simple hellos, and friendship were sent and transmitted. As her son, I was made a part of those numerous conversations, and of course, it would be noted how I had grown since the last time we had met or wasn't I just so proud of my mother for what she had done for some community group or what that person would tell you about how they felt so proud to know her. Respect and affection poured from those people and it flowed like a river of pride over her children. We were the lucky beneficiaries of the attention she garnered from so many, many people. Besides, the food was great, too! Thanks, Mother, for the lesson in respect, said and unsaid. Thanks for the experience of the Depot Grill. Years later when I was in my late 50s, I took my wife back to the Depot Grill so she could experience in some small way part of my childhood. She was amused by the ruggedness and down-to-earth nature of the diner known as the Depot Grill, but also recognized in it one of the many places that shaped the man she knew. On the bulletin board as we left were several pictures of the old days in the Twin Falls area. One of the pictures was of an old junk yard across the street that still has one faded corrugated wall with the partial name "L. L. L_ _ _don on it. In one of those pictures on the bulletin board was a woman with a cutting torch, and it was, you guessed it, Mrs. Marian O. Langdon, my mother.

I trust that painting for you the picture of our mother at work in her unusual occupation was fascinating. Painting a picture of her at home and in our community is equally intriguing as she was an unconventional homemaker and citizen.

As you can well imagine being left a widow early in life with six children at home to parent was daunting, let alone having sole responsibility for the business that supported the family. While my sisters and my brothers and I could and did pitch in, she was the matriarch. Besides cooking, and she was a wonderful cook, she took on one duty that will forever be for us a picture of the most dedicated of mothers. It seems like a simple task in today's world, although those of us who do it would perhaps not agree. But compared to how that task was done without today's modern conveniences, believe me it was one that was much more time consuming and physically demanding than today. It was a task that showed her mettle perhaps more than her tenacity at physical work in the scrap metal business. That was the simple, yet not so simple task of getting our clothes cleaned. Let me tell you what was involved, and you'll see why I choose to give emphasis to the description of it, and the life lesson it became for us.

As I have noted, the house we lived in most of our life as children was located a short block away from the warehouse. Because of the limited living space, there was one necessary task that could not be done there. There simply wasn't enough space for a washing machine to clean the clothes. So, always being the inventive one, Mother decided to clean the clothes at the warehouse.

Typically, wash day—actually spread over two or three evenings—was every other week, regardless of hot or cold weather. It was done in a room that had once served as the kitchen and bedroom for our ailing father during the last year of his life. Perhaps her doing the washing there was not only brought about by necessity, but was a retreat that in the quiet of an evening was a place of solace and an opportunity to relive prior years that were good times for her and her husband. Whatever, the room had in it the numerous fixtures and devices necessary for washing and drying clothes for her large family.

First, there was an old cast iron kitchen stove. It was the kind with four round holes on top, each with a circular lid that could be lifted only with a spring-like handle and a scoop end that slid into the round lid and could be lifted to reveal the fire below. The fire itself could be fed with either coal or wood from in-front where two small doors could be let down, and chunks of fuel could be fed as the fire died and needed to be kindled. Mother preferred wood as a source of fuel, probably because of her days camping on the Little Wood River. The heat that was generated from the stove was tremendous, and the task of approaching the stove to add kindling or put pans and pots on its top required caution lest you be burned by the searing heat. As brother Buzz learned one day, a flame could easily catch you and burn your tender skin. On occasion, the same cast iron stove was used for cooking, like the many times we seared venison strips right on top with a little salt. But most of the time the stove served a very special need, one that is far different than today and so far removed in time that the memory of it has long faded in the lexicon of today's modern conveniences.

The primary purpose of the cast iron stove was to heat the water for washing clothes. Getting hot water wasn't like today where you can get on-demand hot water from your water heater for washing clothes or dishes. You had to heat your own water supply and transfer that to your washing tub or machine if you had one. There were no detergents that would work in cold water like we have today! In my mother's case, she heated the water in two large copper containers, each with wooden handles on the top ends. The two kettles were about 2 feet by 16 inches and were 18 inches deep. They each could contain about 8 gallons of boiling water. As the fire was stoked to its maximum temperature, the water would eventually reach its boiling point, as steam gusted from the top like we used to see in the sulfur pools at the Yellowstone National Park that we visited a couple of times in our youth. You had your water ready, and now came the need to transfer it to the washing tub.

Transferring hot water was accomplished by using a large gallon pot with a long handle on it. She would scoop the pot into the boiling water and with a smooth turn and stroke, transfer it six feet across the room to a waiting wash tub. This was repeated several times until enough hot water was transferred there, and some cold water was added if needed to assure enough water to wash a load of bed sheets, shirts, socks, pants, underwear, dresses, and other assorted items. Into the water also went a bar of Ivory or other soap.

Of course, whites were washed only with whites, and perhaps presoaked with Clorox as needed. Colored clothes were never washed with whites, as this was before the days of colorfast fabrics. Lingerie and other delicates were hand-washed using a washboard. For those not familiar with a washboard, it's a wood-framed device about 24 inches by 14 inches that frames a metal corrugated plate. Placed in a sink or bucket with one end up against your stomach while bracing the legs in the sink, you push your wet and soapy clothing up and down and along the ridges of the metal to literally scrape the dirt off. It is labor intensive, and your arms ached from the constant up and down motion; in and out of the soapy water and then repeated in rinse water. You had to lean over the board, and so your back would begin to ache as well. Even the end supporting the washboard fit tight on your stomach and pushed at you as you scrubbed, providing some unintended exercise—just think, a precursor to today's "abs" exerciser. This form of cleaning clothes was only one step above the native women of Africa and India where I witnessed women washing their clothes on the rocks of river banks.

The task of washing had only begun. Occasionally, she would take a wooden paddle-like device and swirl the clothes around as they washed. If there were stained clothes, and boys had a special way of providing these, she further used the scrub board and those wavy lines of metal that somehow, with gentle strokes and plenty of Ivory soap, got out the stains before entering the clothing into the cauldron of hot water for washing. If that wasn't sufficient to remove stains, then a scrub brush with long bristles, much like the one she used on us when we bathed, would loosen the toughest of stains.

Once the clothes appeared clean they had to be rinsed with clean water, and that required more hot water and a separate tub. Then, they had to be wrung-out using a hand-cranked "wringer." The wringer had two large rubber rollers, much like two bread-dough rollers that squeezed together with enough force to get out most of the water. Sometimes a long or particularly thick piece of clothing would get stuck in the wringer or its side mechanism, and you'd be forced to back the clothing out or disengage the ringer from its side mounting and start again. You had to feed each item of clothing through the ringer separately, perhaps more than once. It often seemed that the ringer added more wrinkles to the clothing, leading one to wonder if the act of getting the water out was of less value than the task it would make of ironing the same wrinkles later.

By this time, the average person would be too weary from the stages of heating water, transferring it, doing the washing and wringing out the clothes to even think that any more stages were needed. Remember, like today, clothing must be dried. You didn't, as we do today, simply put the now-clean and still-wet clothes in a dryer with some nice fresheners to remove wrinkles. Rather, you hung the clothes with wooden clothes pins on a clothes line in the backyard of the house. Even I can remember the difficulty of spreading out wet clothing that stuck together, lifting them to the clothes-line five feet off the ground, and fastening them with the wooden-clothes pins that you held in your mouth. It was heavy and hard work at its best. Imagine what it was like on cold winter days. You didn't put wet clothes outside on the line, for to do so meant they would freeze like some cardboard structures that would never dry until the warmth of the sun made its presence felt. Rather, you folded out several wooden drying racks—sort of Don Quixote-windmill-like structures—throughout the only heated area in the warehouse, and thereon hung the wet clothes. This was the same, but now even-more-cramped room with the coal stove used to heat the water for washing. For larger items like bed sheets and pants, Mother had fashioned hooks from the ceiling. These items would be suspended like ships' sails and would drip until dry on anyone or thing below them. Clothing placed to dry on wooden racks or suspended from the ceiling might take hours or minutes depending on the season of the year and the temperature of the ever present inferno where the water was being heated. The sheer tenacity required to do the wash week after week makes you realize how lucky we are today! As I came to be with her so many times and watched her there in the solace of her duty as she saw it, it's no wonder that my love and admiration for her was ever the so much more instilled and would never be forgotten. I'd be remiss if I didn't also thank my sisters for the countless shirts they ironed for me and the rest of the family. Given what I know today as a man, I feel guilty that the boys didn't share more in the grueling work of cleaning and ironing clothes that was considered woman's work in that day. What a stupid notion by today's standards. It's no wonder that my sister Lucille one day sought the relief afforded by an electric washing machine for our mother though a very special act of love on her part for her mother. More on that later.

The lesson of respect would not be complete without mention of our mother's respect for the environment. I think valuing the world—our environment—is fundamental to respecting yourself and others, and I know she did as well. When we were growing up, the state of Idaho had some large, white, painted letters written on most of the highways one traveled on. I don't know that these slogans written in large letters exist anymore on the highways there today, but I can tell you they were messages of respect for one's environment that Mother took seriously. I know that because she would repeat on more than one occasion the words they spelled out during each trip we took throughout the state. They said things like, "Keep Idaho Green" or "Don't Be A Litter Bug." I've kept this lesson learned from her through those signs, and when I see the litter upon our roads and in parking lots, I wonder who does and does not understand respect for others, let alone themselves? Lucky my mother isn't around, or she would have told you what she thought!

Lesson 4:
Be Nice to Others

My mother probably introduced me to more people than I have personally met on my own in any ten-year span of time. That was because I was often around during her business activities, in the community with her as part of her many service organizations, or dining in the Depot Grill. This also included, certain social events where she never gave a second thought to including one or more of her children. One social event in particular stands out from the many others.

I always chuckle when I think of how many pinochle card games I went to with her when I was nine to twelve years of age, just because she wanted me to come along. For those who don't know the card game of pinochle, it is a four-person game pitting partners against one another. In this case, her group was a regular group of twenty-four women; so there were typically 6 tables of 4 women. All were housewives, except for Mother and a teacher or two, and they met once a month on a rotating basis at each player's house. In addition to playing cards for three or four hours, refreshments such as cookies, cakes, and occasionally ice cream were served, along with enough conversation and gossip to fill a lifetime.

Of course, I was the only man, really a boy. Often there was a woman missing to make a foursome, so they would have me sit in. I got to know most of the women pretty well. The game was what I would describe as friendly, but competitive, with scores kept for prizes that would be given out at the end of several rounds. I won many odd prizes like ash trays, various china pieces, lacy doilies, painted figurines, and so forth. I know my skill had something to do with it, but often as not they were talking so much and I said so little, that I am sure I was the only one paying attention to the card game itself. I used to ask Mother why older people didn't hold their cards up so others couldn't see them. This habit didn't hurt any in my ability to best them at playing the game. Mother's reply was a classic example of her moral stance on things in general. "If you were half-way honest, you wouldn't look!" As I was to understand later in life, the point of card playing and many other experiences was not the prizes—as nice as the pot holders and such were—but rather what we learned about being nice and respectful to others in social circumstances and other public events. When you are in the midst of twenty or so women, all thirty to fifty years older than you, believe me, you mind your tongue and manners if you have any character, let alone the fact that my mother was close by at another table.

Throughout all the years of childhood we were always, always, introduced to others by their last name, preceded by either Mr. or Mrs. or Miss. It wasn't that we didn't also hear and know their first name, but whether an old friend or a newly introduced person, she always in turn introduced me and my brothers or sisters by our first name, and the adult by their last name. It was Mr. Y or Mrs. X or Miss Z! I knew to call them by that title and no other. I would not get punished for any transgression on this rule, mind you. Rather, it was a simple, implicit respect for your elders that was expected. Today, I know things are different and that the neighbor kids call me by my first name and I accept that as being okay. But, it makes me wonder if Mother wasn't onto something that is fundamental about how we look upon and treat others, especially our seniors.

Elders were people, and once introduced, you were expected to say "hello" and carry on some conversation. For me, that was very hard because I was a shy, quiet boy. But gradually, the experience of interacting got easier and easier, and I learned things about others that I would not have learned otherwise. I learned that even if I could not carry on with a topic, I could at least ask a question and that would carry with it all the appearance of a conversation. As we grew in experience, we saw how very important the respect between senior and youth is for both parties. Having visited many senior centers, I have often seen the power of youth for the mind, soul, and body of seniors who long for interaction, and just a small modicum of attention from others. Additionally, lately I've also discovered the great value of music through some guitar playing I've mastered and offered to seniors. You should see their eyes light up. Frankly, most senior centers would do well to be combined with day care for children and other youth activities. Take your own child to see a senior center or retirement home and see what happens! My mother did so on many occasions with me in hand, and I continue to be rewarded by doing so on my own to this day.

Equal in status to properly referring to elders by respectful title are the words, "Thank You." Frankly, I can't recall my mother ever asking, "Did you say, 'Thank You,' Danny?" Rather, I do remember her always saying, "Thank you." By her example, I knew that was what kind people did. She had a look on her face and a way of saying thank you that had genuine sincerity from those two simple words. I am certain it came from the recognition that she had so little in the beginning, that anything, big or little, was a cause to be thankful, and that this would only be known to others if she spoke in genuine and oft-said terms. "Thank you!" was a mantra of her being with others and example to us. Equally so, I found that my mother also had many more non-verbal ways of saying thank you.

During the time my brothers, sisters and I were in grade school at Lincoln Elementary there was always an annual picnic. While the school met as a whole in the local park for this event, each separate homeroom class was responsible for organizing its part of the picnic. That meant that each class had to decide what it would bring, as it was not an activity where you brought your own lunch, but was a group effort. Thus, who would bring sandwiches, chips, plates, glasses, potato salad, and so forth? It was obvious to me that Mother liked school because she always gave us kids the permission to volunteer that she, through us, would provide the sodas—soft drinks to those who don't know that they were called sodas in those days. That meant for our individual home room about three cases of Coke, Orange, Squirt, and certainly Pepsi in a big old galvanized tub full of ice. This is not an advertisement, but Pepsi Cola was our family drink, and it was often said that we perhaps had more Pepsi in our bloodstream than blood itself. I never said Mother had the best information when it came to diet, but then you know, not one of us ever had much in the way of health problems, dental concerns, or illness in general. Thanks, Mother, for the great genes.

I can tell you from personal experience that providing the drinks for outings put you at the top of the heap among your schoolmates. It was a simple act, and I know it wasn't done to impress, but rather to say thanks to the teacher and the school. And if it wasn't the annual picnic she supported, then it was being room mother in every class for each of us, or providing the Stetson hat boxes on Valentine's Day for the class to decorate as the mailbox for their cards to be shared with others in the class, and the special treats for Halloween, ensuring that everyone in the our classes had something. When several of us kids were in Lincoln Elementary at the same time, it was not unusual for our mother to drive up in her pickup at noon time with a huge sack filled with goodies for our lunch, including bananas that peeked over the top of the paper bag. There would often be some extra special treats in your lunch sack to share with someone else. It wasn't difficult, under such circumstances, to find someone to have lunch with, considering the possible advantages of what might be in the bag.

Mother believed strongly in education, no doubt because of her own love of learning and because her own schooling was cut short. She must have really believed in education since she not only educated herself, but also paid for all of her children's college educations, including graduate school for yours truly. We each acknowledge that we were the lucky recipients of her love for education and direct support of all activities related to education.

From the description of our environment, it should be evident that the town that we grew up in, and of which my mother was such a large part, combined to be the best of places to live in and the best of times. It was small enough to get around in, but big enough to have a great variety to things to do. It was small enough to feel safe and to get to know people in. And, even though we lived on the "other side of tracks," we had the whole community as our playground.

All of us children walked to school during the six years of elementary school, three years of junior high, and most to the high school as well. I would have walked to high school, but by that time a new high school had been built about three miles on the other side of town. The elementary school was only six blocks away, and so that was a piece of cake. It was located just past the old Sears building, and you had to cross over the Main Street of town to get to the school. Going to and from the elementary school was pretty routine. On the way home, we often stopped at the Home Market owned and operated by the Larsens, old and trusted friends of our mother's. Back in those days, a penny's worth of candy filled a whole sack and was quite a thrill. When I went into junior high school I walked about eight blocks in a different direction and passed through the main part of the business section of downtown. In the 1950s, Twin Falls, with a population of around eighteen thousand, had one of those typical downtown areas of most small cities. Everything was laid out on a grid, with stores on either side of the two main, intersecting streets that made up the downtown core. Small stories dotted each available space and included the hardware, shoe, clothing, and various other retail establishments. Of course today's malls and big stores have destroyed these typical downtown areas, but in those days they were the center of commerce, where the community of people congregated, and where children could wander with impunity.

There were two stores owned by particular proprietors that I got to know as a child, and each had a strong influence on my life. Mother knew them both, and there was no question ever about my hanging around their establishments on many occasions, especially after school. I can recall instances the owners received a phone call asking if I was there. Or, they might call and ask my mother if it was okay for me to stay a while longer and visit. She was always assured that I was welcome, and confident in the knowledge that I was safe and well taken care of.

One of these establishments was owned by one, Morrie Roth. Mr. Roth owned one of the local shoe stores in town, of which there were three stores at most. A former teacher, he was Jewish, and certainly had a way with words. He would talk your ear off about this and that time he had done such and such, as well as what he believed in politically. And, he asked you lots of questions about everything under the sun. He spoke frequently of how lucky I was to have a mother like mine. He seemed to be fascinated by her as an unusual women in an unusual line of work, but it was her character that he addressed more than what she did. I used to stop by his store on the way home and say hello and just listen most of the time.

Those were the days when they had a machine in the shoe store to see if your shoes fit properly. It wasn't until many years later that we learned that it was an early version of an X-ray machine. It was a tall, box-like device, with a rectangular hole at the bottom, through which you could stick your two feet with the shoes on that you were thinking of buying. You leaned over and looked with both eyes through a scope, at the end of which you could see the outline of your foot bones and the thick outer lining of your shoes with the nails and stitching. To get the machine to operate, you pressed a button and the humming glow of the greenish light made it easy for you and the salesman to see if your new shoes fit, and if not, another pair could be tried and retested in the machine. As I stood there listening to Mr. Roth, I would retest my old shoes repeatedly and was fascinated by what I saw. Given what we know about the dangers of X-Rays, it's a wonder to this day that my feet don't glow in a greenish tint in the dark and haven't fallen off. But it was what Mr. Roth taught me, in his own way, about the plight of the Jews that intrigued me, and the respect he had for other people in general that I best remember; not that shoe machine. He was a bit of a father figure and a bit of a comic, always the one to have a new joke to tell. Though he eventually lost his business as a result of competition from the new mall at the edge of town, until his death, he had a special way of making you feel really good about yourself. I will never forget Morrie Roth.

A second, really interesting person I got to know as a child was Mr. King, the only black man in town, so far as I knew. His full name was Randolph King. He was a great guy, and I loved to stop and talk to him on the way home from Jr. High School. He operated the local shoeshine shop that was nestled between what I recall to be a general appliance store and a card and gift shop. Mr. King had one of those infectious smiles, and he could talk about anything. He told great stories and jokes that I didn't always understand, and he would in turn wonder why I didn't get the point. The main thing was that he was just good to me. The fact that he was black didn't make any difference to me and not to anyone else in town that I could tell. He was part of the community, and as such deserved and received the same respect as anyone else. According to Mother, a person was to be judged by their actions, not their ethnicity and not by what they did for a living. Certainly my mother was of that type. Like Mr. King, she was different from the norm: a women in business and a single mom. Thanks to Mr. King for the lesson in race relations. Whether it was the migrant Mexicans who represented the major "minority" in Twin Falls County, the Japanese interned at the local camp during the war, or the Basque sheep herders, they were the same as anyone else. As I faced issues and experiences in racial strife during the 1960s while a graduate student, those lessons in equality and justice learned as a child in Twin Falls, Idaho, served me well in knowing how to deal with the bigotry that I saw and condemned, and marched and stood-up against. We always knew that had she been there with us, Mother would be marching right beside us and supporting those in need of tolerance and understanding.

As previously mentioned, there were hundreds of men and women who frequented our mother's place of business. Most were clients dropping off scrap to sell, some were old friends not seen for ages, and still others were the curious who were looking for that special thing for their pet project at home. One of these characters was a gentleman named R.S. Tofflemire. Mr. Toffelmire, then the publisher of the only newspaper in town, the Twin Falls Times News, was a true gentleman. For me he served as a model of what being a gentleman meant. Mr. Tofflemire dressed impeccably, always had a neat and clean appearance, right down to polished fingernails. But more pertinent to the story, he was an avid scavenger and a tinkerer. He loved all things mechanical, especially those that had potential for becoming a new creation made from the junk. In my young boy's imagination, he built all kinds of gadgets that could fly, spin around, make noises, and transport you. He seemed to see in a small spring extracted from the innards of an electric motor a link to a device of his imagination. Or, it might be a small strand of electric wire that would connect old, but now newly-configured devices and provide the flow of energy to drive his new creation. You could find him two and three times a week, always neatly dressed in a white shirt and tie, wandering through the Place like some detective looking through eye glasses at the end of his nose for an illusive clue. His well dressed appearance and the jumble of dirty junk he dearly loved was a study in contract, elevating the junk to a higher and more noble place in the scheme of things. There was a constant flow of engine valves, armatures, nuts, bolts, screws, and motors of various kinds that caught his eye. And then he'd as quickly move on to the next item to be scrutinized, eventually gathering a handful of items for which he wanted to check the purchase price. He and Mother would talk for a while, catching-up on one another's lives, and agree upon some price for the assorted items. Many times I heard my mother say, "Oh, just take that thing along," as she gave him a special deal for his regular and repeat business. We never learned what he did with all the stuff he bought, but we did learn about the man. He was kind, an accomplished and well respected newspaperman, reserved, and the model of a perfect gentleman. He never swore, always inquired as to what I was up to and how Mother was doing. Or he would ask how school was going or what was I doing that day. He would pick up something interesting as we walked to leave the warehouse and ask what I thought of it.

Mr. Tofflemire was but one of at least six men that wandered about the yard on occasion, and from which I could glimpse mature and desirable male behavior. I guess you could say Mr. Tofflemire was the first professional-level person I ever encountered. As to the others, there was the farmer who always wanted to give me a quarter just so that I could buy something, but I didn't take the money since I hadn't earned it myself. There was the man who knew baseball in and out and was a Yankee fan through and through. There was a man I worked for a couple of summers as an apprentice electrician, and the blue collar supervisor at an ice cream factory during another summer job. Each of these men, like Mr. Roth, Mr. King, and Mr. Tofflemire were called Mr., and each had a story and a manner indicative of their fine character. I also knew their behavior around me showed respect for my mother in that extraordinary business known as scrap metal, hides, wool, furs and pelts.

Regarding respect, on more than one occasion Mother had an interesting way of responding when someone was disrespectful. She had her limit for those who didn't show respect to her, her friends and certainly to her children. For example, there was the time that sisters Lucille and Bertine were driving back with Mother from a dance recital featuring a well-known ballerina Lucille wanted to see her because of her interest in dance—a career that she would later pursue as a teacher herself for more than forty years. The recital was held in Idaho Falls, a city about 140 miles from our home town. On their return home, they drove along the narrow, two-lane highway between Hansen and Twin Falls, and Mother commented that some man was tailgating her car. Confirming Mother's observation, Bertine, seated in the back seat, had a bird's eye view of the tailgating that went on for several miles. Mother continued to monitor what was going on in the rear view mirror for several miles. Due to approaching darkness and the narrow road, she became ever more cautious as she approached the city limits of Twin Falls. Just as she reached the old cemetery that exists even today, she pulled the car off the road and into the United Oil Company gas station that once was located there. The man in the car also pulled off the road and stopped right behind them. With that, Mother instructed the girls to go into the station and call the police. She, meanwhile, walked back to the man's car, reached in and grabbed the keys, and threw them in the bushes. The tailgater was so stunned that by the time he reacted, my mother and sisters were on the road again. There were times you just didn't mess with our mother; certainly not when you had done something really stupid. I once heard that "being loved makes you strong," and that "loving someone makes you brave." Our mother was a very brave woman.

On another occasion, her actions had more far-reaching implications. She often showed her concern and bravery for others outside her family, and in so doing it was in line with her overall view of right and wrong. One summer day Bertine and Mother were on their way out of the house to do some errands. Bertine had gone out to sit in the car while Mother was retrieving from the house a last-minute item she had forgotten. When Mother exited the back door, Bertine watched her mother abruptly stop on the back step and observe a man and child walking in the alley that ran past our backyard. They could be seen walking in front of an old, run-down, sometimes-occupied small house across the alley from our back door. While a strange assortment of characters had lived in this shack of a house over the years, at this time the house was unoccupied. Mother never said later how, but there was apparently something in the walk and manner of this seeming father and daughter combination that didn't seem right to her. Perhaps it was the way they held hands in what seemed an uncomfortable manner, or it was the pull of his arm on the little girl's hand as if struggling to walk. Whatever it was, Mother came down off the backdoor steps where she was observing, walked decisively over, stopped them, and inquired of the child if the man was her father. The child replied, "No!" and went on to explain that the man had given her some candy and to come with him if she wanted more. At that, Mother took the child by the hand and instructed her to come with her. Seeing this, the man in question started to run down the alley and onto the street. Outside a garage just at the end of the alley, Mother saw someone she knew and yelled to him to catch the fleeing man and he did. In this instance, to be found in the Congressional Record I am told, and in many others, our mother was a staunch defender and advocate for children. She never seemed to operate out of fear of adverse consequence to herself and she never failed to do what she knew was right. It was as if any child was her own and required her protection, care, and love when in danger or need of any kind.

There were many other such unforgettable incidents and stories of Mother's many escapades. As a child and later as an adult, it was like reading the headlines from a daily newspaper when you heard the next unusual thing she had done in her life. Each story and incident had its lasting impact on us children. One of these made me almost drive off a road in disbelief, but also great pride.

It was 1979. I had just returned to Idaho as an adult with my own family after being away from the state for 18 years. During my time away from Idaho I had spent two years in the Peace Corps, a year of graduate school at New York University, a year of teaching chemistry in a high school in Park Ridge, New Jersey, four years working in California and another 10 years in Pennsylvania. After traveling and living in different parts of the world and America, it was strange coming back to the state where I had grown up. Boise was not the same as the town I had spent my years growing up in, and things seemed different, or were they?

I had been in town only a couple of months, when one morning I was driving towards my place of work, the old Morrison Knudsen Corporation offices near downtown Boise. I distinctly remember to this day that I had made my way to within three blocks of my office and was just about to turn the corner onto Broadway Street from Main Street. I was listening, as I usually did, to the news on the local radio station KBOI. The news announcer had given the international report, had covered the state and local news and sports, and was finishing with a local human interest story. He was describing how a 66-year-old woman had the day before detained two would-be robbers who were trying to steal some items from her business. She was seated in a restaurant—yes, the Depot Grill—just across the street, when she looked out and saw these two fellows trying to make off with some items. Seeing them, she walked across the street, confronted them with her questions about their intentions, and not satisfied with their answers told them to just stay where they were until she called the police. They did! As the announcer was finishing the story, I distinctly remember saying out loud to myself, "That's my mother he is talking about!" No sooner had I said that, than he continued his commentary, "Yesterday, 66-year-old Marian Langdon, owner of a Twin Falls scrap metal business, apprehended two would-be thieves and held them until authorities arrived." I almost drove off the road, but I was not, on the other hand that surprised. She always had a sense of what was right and what wasn't. Even though I would not recommend her way of reacting to things in today's world, her actions speak volumes about what we should do towards injustices in our world today. Stories like these about her deeds were not all that uncommon. Her behavior was so consistent that tales of her deeds were common.

A few years later, after the incident I just described, Mother was visiting our sister Lorraine in Maryland. As the story goes, out back on the deck of my sister's house on a moonlit night, Lorraine and Mother could hear two voices, a male and female arguing angrily about something in a nearby home. In the moonlight Mother could make out that a man was holding a knife and was waving it violently about. Without skipping a beat, Mother went running out the back door towards the couple and confronted them about what was going on. It turned out the man had been drinking and was threatening his wife. Most likely startled at Mother's sudden presence, the couple stopped arguing, and Mother returned to the house as if nothing had ever happened. Our mother had a profound respect of herself and for other people. When she saw danger, she acted swiftly, sure of herself and the rightness of her action. She didn't swear, yell or scream, but used a firm voice. She called authorities when needed. People responded to the respect she had for herself. I am not sure how involved she would be personally in today's more dangerous times, but I know she would never turn her back if an act of justice were needed for her own welfare, a stranger, and certainly her children or another child. Perhaps there are not enough role-models like her today that would help control to some degree the street violence, let alone the other injustices that prevail in our society.

In closing the lesson learned about respect for others and yourself, I think it important to note that I never heard Mother ever swear. I think there is some significance to that. Not swearing is a sign of being able to cope in a calm and effective way. It is a lesson I should have learned better myself. I respect that she demonstrated such restraint. I don't know how she did it so consistently, because she certainly faced some bad characters and situations that most people would have liked to swear out loud about. I guess her way was to act with personal restraint based on deep self-respect rather than using easy words that would inflame rather than solve things.

Lesson 5:
Your Brothers and Sisters
Are Your Brothers and Sisters

I was 55-years-old, and I'll never forget the day I learned that there were nine siblings, despite my life-long belief that there were eight children in the Langdon clan. One would think that, as the last child, I would have known how many brothers and sisters I had, but in our unusual family there were always new things to be learned.

It was on the occasion of my brother Archie's death at the age of 75. With 20 years between us, Archie and I were the best of brothers, with that kind of unusual bond where you connect on every level of your being. We hunted and fished together when I was growing up. It was great to have a big brother when I was a teenager and a young man going to college and still in need of occasional guidance from a male figure. He knew how to cook the best buttermilk pancakes in the world, and they always tasted really good when we got up before the sun at 4:00 or 5:00 a.m. and drove to our favorite spot down in the Snake River Canyon just below Buhl. During some of my junior-high-school days, I also often ate lunch at his house, and had a seat at the table of his family's home. When he died, I knew that I had lost forever a brother who was just as much a father-figure as he was my brother.

At his passing, we had gathered, as families do, and at the time we were all seated in the living room of my sister-in-law's just after the funeral, enjoying the usual food and conversation that follows a memorial service. On a table was a copy of his obituary. It was both sad and a reflection of his life to read his obituary, but when I read he was one of nine children my jaw dropped open and I switched from sadness to bewilderment. I immediately brought that apparent error to the attention of the assembled relatives. What followed was a bit mind boggling, to say the least. My sisters Dorothy, Lucille and Bertine said, "No, that's correct!" Only my sister Lorraine, the nearest to me in age, agreed with me and said, "You are right, there are only eight siblings." It turned out, unbeknownst to me and at least one sister, we indeed did have another sibling. I was 55 years old and just learning this new fact!

You may recall in describing our father and his first wife I mentioned that they had a first daughter that died at the tender age of nine months. It turned out that it was not so uncommon in those times, due to the high mortality rate among infants, that when a baby child died, little was said after the death. Was it too much to bear or was it so common that to dwell on it would cause undue suffering? It was as if death might be expected, but when it occurred there was denial, or perhaps a fundamental need to move on and take care of remaining children. It was also not uncommon that when a child of the same sex was born later, that child received the name of the child that had died earlier. In our family's case, our parents did apparently talk about the death of the first child for some years, thus the three older children of Father's first wife and the three oldest children born of our mother and father knew of the child's death, but after that it wasn't mentioned again. So Buzz, Lorraine, and I had no idea that we indeed had an older sister, because everyone else stopped talking about it. After learning this startling fact so late in life, I made a point to refer to being part of a family of nine, although it has slipped off my tongue at times that there were eight of us; then I have corrected myself, much to the bewilderment of others. "No, I am sorry there were nine of us." You get that kind of look which says, how in the world wouldn't you know how many brothers and sisters you have? Sorry about that, but that is my predicament.

You may have noted throughout the book that I refer to all of my brothers and sisters as my brother or sister and never use the phrase step-brother or step-sister. I don't like writing that "step" prefix even here. I do so at this point only to make a point of practice in our family regarding our maternal and fraternal relationship. There was an unwritten rule in our family that you never used the words "stepchild," "stepbrother," or "stepsister." The only exception to this rule was when someone wanted to know why one of your brothers or sisters was so much older than you, or how you could have a niece that was two years older than you were. I am convinced that habitual way of referring to family members went a long way in insuring that we perceived one another with an unquestioning sense of equality and respect of one another. And, indeed, in practice we got the same treatment from our mother whether "stepchild" or biological child. Having respect for your bothers and sisters is not, of course just a matter of saying you will respect one another and referring to one another in equal terms. It has to be promoted in tangible ways. Our respect and loyalty to one another was a practice our parents expected of us, and acceptable reference to one another as equal brother and sister was just the beginning standard. What we did with one another and how we played were other practices that brought family togetherness and respect of one another. A few other examples will demonstrate how.

Like any teenager, my brother Buzz went many places with his own friends. I am certain he didn't expect that his baby brother would tag along. However, Mother, under the right circumstances, would ask if he would take me along. Mother, likewise, expected at times that of our sisters in their relationship with one-another. I guess because my brother Buzz was the closest brother in age to me by some three years, it naturally fell upon him to take me along at times when I am sure he would rather have been alone with his friends. But that was the way it was to be, and he respected his mother too much to do otherwise, or argue the point. I suppose if Mother had known that my brother Buzz smoked cigars with his friends at the age of 15, she might have thought better of it. But I am sure that little bit of foolishness was far less important than the lesson he learned in having responsibility for his younger brother. And I learned the safety of being with a brother, let alone the things he taught me like how to tie an artificial fly on the end of your fishing line to do some fly fishing. There is a special technique to such fly tying, and while it can be learned from a book, having it passed from father to son, as our father had done for him, and then him to me, since our father had died, it was special to have learned it from my brother. Mother made sure these experiences were made possible by assuring we were linked as children in common experiences. Likewise, on other occasions, my brother took me and taught me swimming with him and his friends, and I accompanied him and the team as the batboy for a trip to the state baseball tournament. There were many other times Mother orchestrated our togetherness. In our family, you just looked out for and learned from one another! Blood may be thicker after all! Our mother was big on promoting responsibility, and taking care of one another was just one of the ways she made sure you were responsible.

We were children of a family who played together. We didn't have television in those days, so I guess that was part of the reason, but I'd like to think it had to do with just enjoying one another. Often our mother could be found in the center of the activity or event, although she was just as comfortable watching from the side lines. For example, we played kick-the-can together into the setting sun by the street lamp outside on the corner near our house. We played all kinds of board games—Monopoly was often the game of choice. It was, however, playing the card game known as Pinochle that got us really going in a highly-spirited way. We would play hand after hand, day and night, and the competition was keen. Usually, the game went pretty smoothly and the winning was evenly passed around enough that no one felt a lack of achievement for all the healthy competition. But there were times when emotions could run high. When it came to playing Pinochle, this was especially true for our sister Lucille. She'll kill me for telling this story, but when she had had enough frustration of our beating her at the game, she would unceremoniously toss all her cards high into the air. They would shower down upon the table, effectively ending the game and sending the rest of us into complaints that she had spoiled the game, and we were "ahead" at the time. In retrospect, it wasn't the competition of the game that was important, nor even winning. Rather, it was just being together as a family. We thank Mother for bringing us together to play and for all the other activities of togetherness she orchestrated that made us a family.

One of the keys of getting along with one another was our use of humor in our family. Indeed, if you didn't develop a sense of humor in our family, you were certainly in for plenty of ribbing from the others. Fortunately, every child developed, in varying degrees, a sense of humor. Humor is not just a giving thing. We learned that if you are going to give it, you had better know how to take it. Humor is the art of both giving and receiving, and if you learn it the right way, you "roll with the punches," as the saying goes.

The humor in the Langdon family is that brand where you can generate a quick retort to virtually anything that is said. The retort may even seem like a putdown, but it is never at the level of being personal such that one's feelings are hurt. And if you give it, you had better expect to take it in kind. It's very much like the mutual respect athletes have for one another's skill level, while constantly trying to outperform the other. It's close to dueling comedians who know that each can top the other, but never outright win. Mother found it truly amusing, if not amazing, that we could use so much humor, but she seldom participated. Her response was almost always the same; she would simply say, "Oh, you kids!" and she would laugh and shake her head. It was her way of delighting in us, but especially because of our getting along with one another. Also, I think her not participating was deliberate, lest she appear to be trying to outdo her own children. We thank you, Mother, for the opportunity to be ourselves and to share mutual love though humor.

I have come to realize that developing a sense of humor was a key ingredient to becoming a healthy adult. It helps not only in getting along with immediate family, but it was a useful tool in dealing with others as well. I know that in my relationship with my wife, she has said more than once that my brand of humor can easily take the tension off in virtually any kind of disagreement that we have faced. She is fond of telling friends about the time I jumped up and down on the bed in a clowning fashion during a disagreement with her. It simply broke her into so much laughter it made it impossible to argue any further. Apparently there is some recent research that supports the use of humor as a mark of successful marriages. Of course, you have to know how to use humor in a positive way. Believe me that was no problem in our family growing up! Having observed several generations of Langdons, it is nice to see that humor has been passed on to subsequent generations

In the same way that humor was always prevalent, playing jokes on each other was no less so, and Mother could provide her share of "joking around." I believe joking around was simply an extension of humor that said, "Keep things light. Don't take the world so seriously! Have some fun!

I remember one thing that everyone seemed to participate in. You take a pillow and prop it up on the top of a slightly open door. It's placed on the other side of the door from which your mother, brother or sister will be entering; especially at night where they can't see it in the dimly-lit room. When they do open the door, the pillow tumbles down on their head. No matter how often we did it, the "victim" was always surprised—and always laughed at getting caught that way. Sounds kind of corny when you describe it, but it was standard fare for a period of time in our household. If not that, an inverted glass of water using waxed paper to place it on the kitchen counter would certainly do the trick when someone picked up the glass to put it away and the water splashed and startled them. I can't tell you how many times Mother laughed when we put crackers or a piece of fruit in between her false teeth after she had taken them off at night and placed them on the bed stand. When she awoke in the morning, you could hear her laughter from the next room. Her approval of your antics demonstrated her capacity to take, as well as approve of and promote humor. These cat and mouse games of who could out-humor the other in our family were certainly far better than arguing, which we rarely did as a family. Humor represented our mutual love and respect of each other, and became an important mechanism for coping with life's stresses and challenges.

Lesson 6:
Don't Sweat It, Get Over It!

Our mother had some really practical and useful sayings:
"Don't take any wooden nickels"
"There's no one crueler, on occasion, than kids."
"I look like the wreck of the Hesperus."
"The Lord willing and the creek don't rise."
"I look like the last rose of summer."
"More than Carter's little liver pills."
Among all those sayings, I suppose my favorite was: "That's the way things are. That's the way things were meant to be."

Mother was never one for making excuses or complaining about things. She felt that was a way of not facing up to problems that face everyone in one form or another. And complaining was simply an excuse for not having to find a way to move torward the handling of adversity. This philosophy has a certain simplicity to it, but is a powerful way of life. Her example was one of the most valuable lessons given to her children. Given her single-mother status, working every day in a very difficult job in all kinds of weather, washing clothes in the most difficult of conditions, and raising a passel of kids, she was entitled to whine, but she never did. Rather, she felt very blessed.

Feeling sorry for yourself was not tolerated much in our growing up. Mother exuded the notion that doing so was just not worth it. On reflection, I believe her experiences in surviving motivated her to overcome adversity. As such she vowed to never say, "I can't," for to do so would create, in her thinking, self-doubt. Rather, she said, "What am I going to do given the challenges I am faced with?" As a result, things worked out for her because she made them work out for her. Her philosophy was that you learned from your experiences so you are better prepared for future challenges that you will surely face in life. She was right! And she had her ways of letting us know that complaining would not work for you either; instead, it was far better to get on to a solution.

Mother's philosophy of, "Face it, get over it, and move on," manifested itself in all kinds of ways but, there is one classic story that illustrates this lesson as recounted by our sister Lucille.

Lucille was attending the University of California Los Angeles (UCLA) located in Westwood, California. She was majoring in drama, which perhaps explains in part why she reacted the way she did in this story.

Lucille was an outstanding student. She met and married her sweetheart at UCLA, and graduated with honors. So, she had lots going for her. One Christmas break before graduation, she, Mother, and Bob Latham, a hometown friend, were returning from college for a winter break. An incident occurred that forever served as a lesson to Lucille of Mother's view on what is, and what isn't, important and your reaction to it.

They had driven about a quarter of the distance from Los Angeles to Twin Falls, Idaho and had stopped in Reno, Nevada to have dinner. During the stop, the family friend, Bob, had to get something from the trunk of Mother's Buick. When he was finished, he inadvertently left the trunk slightly open. And, off they went down the highway continuing their journey. Well, before too long Mother noticed that the trunk of the car was up, so she stopped beside the road there in the early dusk of the evening. She noted that something that had been on the top of the suitcases was gone. It was a beautiful formal chiffon dress that Lucille was bringing to wear to her old high school's winter dance. She knew she would be stunning when she saw her old high school friends. But it had apparently flown out of the car trunk into the night. Lucille was beside herself with grief over the loss of that formal, but as she began to lament with some tears, Mother stopped her. Right there on the side of the road and in plain and forthright language Mother told her, "Don't let me ever hear you cry over the loss of anything like that again. You can always replace a thing! Crying over spilled milk won't do you any good or get your dress back." Lucille never forgot the lesson. As it turns out, even though they retraced their journey back to Reno, they couldn't find the formal. However, the next day Mother put a lost and found ad in a Reno newspaper. Within a day, a woman called to say she had found the formal and would send it by bus right away. The upshot of the whole incident was that Lucille had the formal in time for the dance and learned that her grief was pretty much for naught. Mother's philosophy was, **"Don't Sweat It, Get over It!"** I have used that as a mantra myself many times to make sure that I am living life and coping with difficulties as adventures, rather than a reason to complain and become immobile. Besides, it frees your body and mind from all that self-imposed stress that ages and disables.

Lesson 7:
Service to Others

I have never had a doubt that my mother was a very special person, but one of her most remarkable aspects was the intense level of service to others she provided. I witnessed many times her service to others through both the sweat and toil of her work and the way she did many things on a personal level for others and for the community as a whole. She had a big heart when it came to doing things for others. A couple of quotes from one of many newspaper article about her service exemplify her willingness to be involved whenever asked or when she saw something that drove her to action:

"Mrs. Langdon was always on call, always ready to put on her jeans and drive up in the big truck and help the children load paper for the war scrap drives."

—Beulah Way, Principal of Lincoln Elementary School

"Mrs. Langdon is always around when young people, by the truckload, need transportation."

—Mrs. R. O. McCall, Director of the Local YWCA

Mother once told me the way she got into being part of so many service organizations and her own personal contact with those in need. She said it began when she was first introduced to the needs of many who were victims of the polio epidemic that struck the United States in the 1950s.

A friend of hers, Frankie Alworth, owner and proprietor of an antique store in town, came by one day and asked her to volunteer at the local Twin Falls Hospital. She herself was doing some volunteer work with victims of polio—that once-dreaded disease that crippled and killed so many. Polio hit especially hard young children, and Mother recalls seeing kids brought in from the outlying towns of Rupert, Paul, and many other communities, including Twin Falls. Several were Japanese children residing in the area with their parents after a local interment camp was dismantled following the Second World War. Most polio victims had to be housed in "Iron Lungs."

Iron Lungs were huge round shell-like encasements that were a support to life's very breath. They encased the whole of the body except for the head and protruding legs. I remember going with my mother to the local hospital and seeing these struggling souls. My sister Lorraine became a practice patient for Mother and her volunteer friends to learn more about patient care. Your heart could not help but sink as you watched the pure agony of relying on a machine to breath for the patient. And, there was the constant bellowing sound that it made as the machine inhaled and exhaled life's very force. It was on one such trip that I decided to get involved myself. It was one of those many instances where a parent sets the example for their children to follow in their own way.

I learned that the ward Mother was working in needed a new phonograph (record) player. There was a small collection of children's records, but the record player had broken a few weeks earlier and there simply wasn't money enough to replace it when funds were so desperately needed for patient care. After checking with the boy scout head scoutmaster, I volunteered my boy scout patrol, of which I was the patrol leader, to find a way to get a new record player for the hospital. The seven members of the patrol decided on a unique, but labor-intensive way to raise money. Over a period of three weeks we went door-to-door and collected hundreds of wire coat hangers. Upon hearing our plan, the local dry cleaning store—the same one where got our burning dirt by the way—agreed to pay us at a penny a piece for every wire hanger we brought in. Given that, we scoured practically the whole community, asking everyone who came to the door to give us their spare clothes-hangers. We collected, sorted, and counted hundreds in packages of 50 each, tied with string. We had enough to buy not only a record player, but several records as well. The local record store then contributed a couple of items on their own. It was a thrill for us to go and present the record player to the hospital, and to witness the children appreciate something they had inspired, but that we had done on our own.

One of the most direct ways we observed Mother helping others was that she lent out to those who needed them, a collection of a hospital beds that she had amassed over several years. I am sure having this supply of hospital beds started when Father became ill during the last year of his life. He had to be confined pretty much to a bed for constant rest and treatment. Before long it became apparent as his body functions changed, that he needed a hospital bed, if not for comfort, then for the conveniences of being taken in an out of regularly. So they acquired one of those traditional hospital beds with the crank handles on the bottom end. This allowed someone to raise and lower the head or bottom of the bed and arrange the person in various angles for different needs. When he died, Mother found herself with a hospital bed on her hands. Not being one to just store it away, she lent it to anyone who might need it. What started as one bed slowly evolved to a collection of several beds lent out for free to all who called. I am sure her early experience in living in a hospital played a role in inspiring her to do what seemed to her the right and natural thing to do for others.

In other instances, she would often ask us kids to accompany her as she distributed bags of food to needy people in the community at Thanksgiving, Christmas, or whenever a need was made known to her. I don't know how she knew about people in need for sure, but she had a network of friends who would tell her. She had her hand on the pulse of the community and especially the plight of others. She would pack several bags of food and clothing items together and we would drive to the home. There she would be greeted with great affection and leave with her own reminder to me of just how lucky we were as a family. "You never know what people need or how they came to be where they are, but when they need help you just have to do something." Again, one has to know that her own early life's struggles played a significant part in this generosity towards others. And there was, of course, her faith-based belief that we were meant to help others when the need called for it.

I suppose if anything was distinguished in Mother's service record, it was the fact that she was the consummate service organization volunteer and leader. And, most of this list was accomplished while she was running her business full time, although she continued well into retirement to be no less active in many causes. I will recount several of her services to others, but I am sure that there were others:

- Chairperson of the March of Dimes
- Vice-President, March of Dimes
- Board Member, March of Dimes
- President of the Twin Falls Business and Professional Women's Club
- President of the State Business and Professional Women's Club
- President of the Soroptimist Club
- President of the 20th Century Club
- Senior Citizens' Board Member, Twin Falls
- Member of the Women of the Moose
- Member of the Magic Valley Memorial Hospital Auxiliary
- Worthy Matron of Magic Chapter No. 82 of Eastern Star
- Worthy Matron of Twin Falls Chapter of Eastern Star
- Worthy Matron of Hollister Chapter No. 49
- Worthy Matron of Lorraine Chapter No. 20 of Eastern Star

- Secretary/Treasurer of Past Matrons' Club
- Guardian of Job's Daughters Bethel No. 19
- Member of Garnet Court No. 3, Order of Amaranth
- Vice President and President of Northwest Association of Bowlers
- Registrar for East New Plymouth Election Precinct
- Member of Priscilla Club
- President of the United Methodist Women of the Payette Church
- Chairman of Annual Christmas Bazaar
- Organizer of rummage sale to benefit church missions
- State President of Idaho State Mothers Association
- Chairperson for several years of Filer Fair Baptist Church Booth
- Classroom mother in our elementary school for 15 years and high school for 2 years
- Secretary, Junior-Senior PTA
- Secretary-Treasurer, City Safety Council
- Member, Chamber of Commerce
- Secretary, Committee for the Physically Handicapped
- Member, YWCA
- YWCA Board Member
- YMCA Board Member
- Sponsored various bowling teams
- Sponsored numerous Little League baseball teams; often the teams called themselves the "Little Scrappers"
- First Vice-President, Twin Falls County Polio Board of the national foundation
- Volunteer for the annual Community Chest
- Volunteer for Boy Scout Campaigns
- First Vice-President, Twin Falls County Polio Board
- Finance Chairperson, First Baptist Church
- First woman to serve on the Board of Trustees for the First Baptist Church
- Member and Volunteer, Hospital Guild
- Vice-President of Public Affairs Committee
- Chairperson for five years of the Idaho Products Dinner
- President, Business and Professional Women's Club

• Director of the South Central District Business and Professional Women's Club
• Chairperson of Public Affairs Committee of the Business and Professional Women's Club
• Vice-chairman of the Twin Falls Chapter of the National Foundation
• Vice-president of Employ the Handicapped in Twin Falls
• Member, Women of the Moose
• Vice-President of the Twin Falls Bowling Association
• Chairperson of the Antique Department of the Twin Falls County Fair
• Member, Magic Valley Hospital Guild

For her volunteer work she received many formal recognitions. Among these were "Woman of the Year" from the Atrusa Club of Twin Falls, and "Member of the Year" from the United Methodist Women of Payette. Her certificates of appreciation and accomplishment number as many organizations as she served and more since she often served on committees and ran programs for several years.

Although she considered all of her activities to be of equal importance, among these the service organization she dearly loved the most is one known as Eastern Star. A description of it here is given not only for her love of the organization, but to make a special point about overcoming adversity and seeking until you triumph. When she saw an injustice our mother was never a quitter, but some times even she needed some help!

For whatever reason, perhaps this organization's emphasis on service to others, she wanted to be a member of the fraternal organization known as Eastern Star. Initially, her attempt to become a member presented a very unexpected challenge and a lesson in just how some people can be. Undaunted, she nonetheless prevailed at becoming what she wanted and in so doing changed an unjust rule that should never have existed in the first place.

Fraternal clubs can have a downside, especially when they have any tinge of discrimination to them. Sometimes it's a national issue and sometimes it's just the bias of local members. I already accounted for my personal experience as an adult with the Boy Scouts of America and their view of gays being in leadership roles. Mother's experience with Eastern Star as a fraternal organization was no less daunting, it served I am sure as a guiding light to my own action towards that organization.

It seemed a little ridiculous to Mother in 1960 that in order to become a member of Eastern Star you had to have a male relative who was already a member of the fraternal organization known as the Masons. She found this out because her son, Archie was a very active Mason of some high degrees and so she applied for membership in Eastern Star. It turned out that someone in Eastern Star didn't think Mother qualified to be a member of their organization because Archie was, in fact her step-son and not her son by birth, and so they "blackballed" her membership. Given what I've already described about her, you can imagine how that sat with my mother. I can tell you that it didn't settle well with her son, Archie, or for that matter with any of us. But she still wanted to join because it was the right thing to do and she would not take no for an answer. So, as much as I generally hated and do to this day dislike being in clubs (other than professionally), I decided to join the Masons and go through their rituals just so that my mother could become a member of Eastern Star. After the few months it took for that to happen, I don't recall ever attending another meeting of the Masons, but she on the other hand went on to be a model member in Eastern Star, holding many offices and sponsoring many activities. She could have been justified to be somewhat bitter towards the group, but it was more important for her to be in service to others. She kept her eye on what was most important! I think it was for her not just a matter of fighting against an injustice as she saw it, but getting inside that organization to see that changes would be made for others that followed, and she did just that. It was also good for me to do something for her even if I didn't personally care to join a fraternal organization. Besides, it was a good lesson to see her tenacity in getting what she wanted no matter how short-sighted others can be. Thanks again for the lessons learned in service to others, no matter how hard it might be to achieve.

Lesson 8:
Doing Things for Your Parents

Wanting to do things for your parents can, of course, come out of a sense of obligation because they are, after all, your parents. When it comes from profound respect for them—a respect they earned by their example—then pure love drives your heart to do things to honor them. Love and respect have always driven us to do things for our mother.

Mother taught each of us to take care of the things you can do yourself before asking others to do things for you. By her own example, Mother would rarely ask us directly to do things for her, which we would have gladly done. Being the self-directed, independent woman that she was herself, she taught us by example to be the same way. My wife knows, for example, that I rarely ask others to do anything I can just as easily do myself. Certainly there are times to ask others for help, but more often than not, lots of self-initiative goes a long way. I think perhaps since she asked for so little, but did so much, we wanted to do more for her.

Of course, as a very little kid I did some strange things for my parents. For example, when I was about 5-years-old I decided to fill the gas tank of my parents' truck, just like I had seen at the local Conoco gas station. In those days, an attendant actually came out and washed your windshield, checked the oil and battery, and filled your tank with gas. As I "pumped" the gas, I also asked my parents if there was anything else I could do. I was emulating the things I saw happen at the gas station, except that I was filling the tank with water from the garden hose. I had the idea of doing something special for my parents and I had a good idea, but there was a problem with the execution. Luckily I was cute, because nothing ever came of it except for their laughter.

If there is one thing I am pretty good at, it is organizing things. To this day it is one of the qualities that my wife admires and appreciates in me. Since Mother was a collector of everything, organization was an area of some expertise in which I could help her.

We never knew exactly why, but Mother was a collector of all kinds of objects. And I mean ALL kinds of things. It might have been because of the junk yard she owned and operated, since the "junk" often revealed a treasure of collectables. We used to have a saying that fit the situation: "Junk Bought; Antiques Sold." From old branding irons to wagon wheels, she saw both beauty, and I think, a sense of history in each item. Who did she imagine came West on those wooden wagon wheels or identified their cattle by one of the unique branding irons she collected? She had at least 300 wagon wheels and at the final count, at least 325 branding irons. And this doesn't touch the number of old irons for taking the wrinkles out of clothing, the "Iron Rests" upon which these irons were placed when hot, electric insulators, old car hubcaps, license plates, hurricane lamps, assorted farm items, and other items of interest she kept. "Junk Bought; Antiques Kept" might have been a better description of her collecting activities!

Her natural curiosity and sense of value contributed to her collecting pleasure. She recognized value that other people missed in a variety of things. She saw value while visiting hundreds of antique stores, or in a hardware store going out of business, the sometime flea market across the street, or items in someone's back yard or in a farmer's barn or field. At the time of her retirement and move to our sister Bertine's farm, it took three semi-tractor trailer trucks to move her household, most of which was her vast collectibles. Living through the experience of the Depression probably contributed more to her collecting passion than anything else. It's hard for those of us who haven't lived during really hard times like the Great Depression to appreciate what our parents or grandparents went through and how that formed their subsequent attitude and approach to daily living. Just surviving was really difficult! For most people, it was literally a question of meeting day-to-day needs. My mother's plight as a child, short-experience as a young adult before marrying at age seventeen, and relatively short period of marriage, may have made her want to be surrounded by whatever she considered an item of beauty or necessity for the future. Many, if not most, people like our mother, after the Depression kept virtually everything that they considered of any value. Perhaps it was pieces of paper to be reused, balls of strings, stacks of old newspapers, odd dishes, countless jars, and odd clothing kept for future use in drawers and boxes in the attic. These possessions, often kept beyond their usefulness, represented a kind of security in the event that hard times should return. Wasting was almost a sin. "Waste not, want not," was a familiar slogan during those times. Cherishing what you had was a way of being grateful. People who went through the Depression were often wiped out; therefore while many of the things they saved after the Depression were of little or no value, at least the things saved were theirs. Some of this habit rubbed off on me from my mother. For example, when I see pennies ignored on the street, scattered and left in the dust, it speaks to me of lack of value placed on what should be valued. It is no wonder Mother collected not just out of a sense of value, but out of an underlying need for security.

Of the many things she collected, one item stands out as very vivid even to this day. Mother had a collection of at least 2,000 pairs of salt and pepper shakers! My sisters are quite accurate on the exact number of shakers, given that they were paid 1¢ for each pair they cleaned on more than one occasion. Most of the more ornate or valuable pairs were neatly displayed in a collection of eight china closets. They were to be found both in our home and in part of the warehouse. Most pairs of salt and pepper shakers, however, were simply kept in empty round apple crates that were stacked in the old living room area of the warehouse that had served as our residence at one time. Since this room was also jammed with lots of other odd boxes and collectibles, you had to climb over the top of some of these apple crates just to get from one area in the room to another. And, I confess to having walked on the apple crates on occasion as a kid. It's a wonder that I didn't break more of them than I did. She never said a word about my behavior and I quickly learned not only to value what she valued, but to get others to value what I valued.

Mother collected not only all kinds of items, but usually in great quantities. She had an eye for both quality and value that would have been an asset in today's televised antique shows. In fact, it seemed to us children that if an item existed, she either had one or knew of it. She was a prolific reader of magazines and catalogues on antiques. Among many other pieces, she had a complete twelve-place setting of Roseville Pottery. I used to joke with her that she was not to leave me any of that pottery in her will. I even jokingly gave her for her 65th birthday a paper-set version of that pottery I found one-day in a party shop. She was quite amused upon receiving it. When she died, I selected one of the finer pieces of Roseville Pottery just to remind me of her and the special bond we had. It is in the entry to my home and welcomes everyone on their arrival. It receives both personal comment and admiration by a son who understands what it represented to the woman who valued it so highly.

On occasion, Mother did sell or trade a few items from her collection. This was especially true upon her retirement when she had more time to devote to her collections. She wasn't a packrat if I somehow gave that impression. She mostly traded or sold because she wanted something else, and a wise trader knows what to keep and what to pass on. She said more than once that, "My collections will never depreciate—they're always worth something." I especially remember the time that she sold something in order to buy a particular item she wanted.

Shortly after she had retired and moved to our sister Bertine's farm, 170 miles north of our home town, near the town of New Plymouth, Idaho, she decided it would be nice to have a hot tub. She wanted it for her aging bones and for her grandchildren who were still around to enjoy. So, using that keen sense of trade she always possessed, even in her retirement, she proceeded to sell off the "odds and ends," as she referred to them, of her 300 piece Roseville Pottery collection. Mind you, she only sold the odds and ends, and yet it was enough to buy a hot tub which she enjoyed for many years. She was astute in assembling and valuing a collection, as well as trading or selling-off things when something else was more important. It truly wasn't merely a sense of having to have things just to possess them for their value. Rather, it was a love of beautiful and fascinating things that simply delighted her. Her collection of things purchased or traded for from others and collected from the scrap metal business included, but was not limited to the following:

- A collection of branding irons
- Some of the finest and fanciest women's hats you ever saw in the style of the 1920s to 1950s
- An extensive cut-glass collection, including Depression glass and Carnival Glass
- Numerous cruets
- Cast-iron cooking pots and utensils
- Old farm items, including a corn husker, grinders, mining pans, cooking utensils, milk/cream separator
- Many patterns of different pottery
- A twelve-place setting of Desert Rose china
- Various types of glass items from soda fountains of the 1940s and 1950s
- Dolls of every size and type
- Farm implements
- Hundreds of wooden-spoke wagon wheels
- Historic and period plate collections
- Sheet music
- Foreign coins
- American stamps
- Books, especially poetry
- Tea sets, enough for each of her 15 granddaughters to receive a set at her passing)
- China closets: (Note: Enough for each child to have at least one at her passing)
- Clippings of newspaper events and pictures that caught her eye
- Match books
- Calendars from the business

As children each of my brothers and sisters did what they could to help their mother. Whatever they did, it was designed and motivated to make her life a little easier or to simply please her in gratitude for all she had done or was doing for her family. If it wasn't helping to dust and organize her many collectibles or something else, then it was making sure, particularly in her retirement she got to do, or have, or see the things she had only dreamed of. She did not take the time or necessarily have the means to do special things for herself while rearing her family, so we did those things for her out of love for her. I know that the simple act of organizing her antiques was something that I liked to do for her, and she, in turn, expressed her appreciation. Or it might be to straighten the ever constant, accumulating things in the tiny house we occupied. Besides, there were so many things scattered here and there, that organizing for an unobstructed passage way was practical, if not a necessity. Or we might cook a special meal or prepare a special desert. Pies were my specialty. We did these things for her from pure love rather than a sense of obligation, and it spoke volumes for the positive and loving lessons she taught us by her example.

It will be possible to detail only some of the special and sometimes mundane things that her children did. The purpose is not to highlight these events just as events, but rather to capture a sense of our love for her and our realization that she was constantly doing for us. It was "small" or "token" repayment, from her children in recognition of her. I also think you will find them fascinating as reflections of individual love. It would take at least eight books to cover each child's acts of love, but a few examples will illustrate just how much we thought of our mother.

For my part I always liked tinkering with and building things. When I was 17 I decided to build her a patio in the backyard of her house. Noting the bare space outside the back door that begged for attention, I hatched a plan. A high school friend and I collected flagstone from the dessert near the side of a canyon wall. When we had collected enough, I neatly placed them in a rectangle, scattered sand between the stones, and placed one of her old wagon wheels in the center as a table. It made a nice place for relaxing with a soft drink, to play some cards, or just sit and enjoy the evening. I am sure she enjoyed watching the construction as much as she enjoyed my completed project. I know she was pleased with my initiative and ability to do the work pretty much on my own. A couple of years later I added a fish pond, complete with an old style water pump, as a complement to the patio. Made from a large metal tank found in the junkyard, it created a lovely place for her to enjoy, while at the same time incorporating some of the scrap metal from her own business.

I also painted the rather extensive fence that surrounded our home and the lot next door, even if I did burn out the vacuum cleaner that I had converted to a paint sprayer. I often dusted and organized the house so that when she came home from a long day's work she would be surprised and pleased. I even put forth some fledgling culinary skills into the making of pies, cakes, tarts and cookies. For those who think these are not things boys do, then I haven't made my point through these stories. I believe love is not just what you feel, but in what you do. I'll close my personal account of doing things for our mother with one more story near and dear to me, as I know it was to her.

When I was in my 50s and she in her late 70s, I asked my mother to think of one thing she had always wanted to do, but had not. Was it go to China and see the Great Wall, or go to Egypt and see the pyramids? Or, perhaps to buy something she always wanted? What was it? I asked. Her answer really surprised me because it was so simple and so reflected her being. She told me that she and my father had discussed on several occasions a particular thing that she had longed to do, but had just never gotten around to. They did lots of things together, but this thing simply slipped through the cracks of a busy life raising their children and work. To understand why she wanted to do this particular thing, you need the understanding of what she valued and what her life was like growing up as I have portrayed here for you in this book. What she finally said she wanted in response to my question, was something quite simple that had great personal meaning to her as if it fulfilled life itself. She had a way about her when it came to such things that perhaps others would not have valued so much. She loved roses for example. She loved going places. She loved the beauty of nature. I think she loved most anything for the sheer adventure of it and could gain from things what many of us might overlook. All things were part of the world that she struggled to survive in as a child and in early adulthood. It was as if that entire struggle in the early years added up not to resentment as it does for many people, but to simple appreciation for everything that was here and was possible. You just had to put your mind to it and it would come to you. I've used that philosophy she believed in to realize I could write books, and so I did. That seeing all possibilities and simplicity in what lays before us if we chose action over inaction, is a fundamental lesson that she taught us through her actions and approach to life. Of all things she could have said to me, this one simple request was a thing of beauty: "I would like to go the Rose Parade in Portland, Oregon!" Mind you, that is not the famous Rose Parade in Pasadena, California which I might well have understood. It was the Rose Parade in Portland, Oregon! With all due respect to the people of Portland, who has heard of their rose parade other than the people in Oregon? Well, my mother had heard of it! That is all I needed to know!

Perhaps the source of information about this particular parade was our father's mother who was from Oregon and had visited on occasion. She probably had described the parade to our mother. Grandmother lived the remainder of her life in Oregon and would certainly have been familiar with it. Father had traveled in Oregon as well and perhaps heard of it and recounted it to her in conversation. For whatever reason it might have been, this was the one thing she still wanted to do. So, on the day before the parade I flew in from California where I was living and picked her up, and we drove over to Portland from New Plymouth, Idaho, where she was living at the time.

I still chuckle to this day when remembering our experience of going to the Rose Parade. For one thing, there was not one rose to be found during that parade. I searched and searched, but other than a rose bush in someone's front yard, we never saw a rose. It made no difference, in that we had a wonderful experience together as we drove to and from Portland, and where we sat and watched the parade. It turned out that the parade is a busy time of the year for Portland and finding accommodations was not easy. I had arranged for a hotel on the outskirts of town, but it was a kind of drizzly, rainy day and that would not do for her special occasion as far as I was concerned. So, the evening before the parade I managed, using that never-give-up-philosophy she had taught me, to find a hotel room that would be available the morning of the parade. Best of all, the hotel was situated on the very corner where the parade would pass before the grandstand where the judges would be reviewing the floats and marching bands. There were all kinds of home-grown floats of papier-mâché depicting local commerce, marching bands, veterans, beauty queens and their courts, and the usual assortment of service organizations. We watched the full parade from our comfortable hotel room through a large window on the second floor right over the parade. We sipped tea and coffee in comfortable chairs. We had the same view as the judges below us on the reviewing stand, and were much more comfortable in the warmth of the room on that rainy day. We even had a TV to watch the parade. The twinkle in her eyes as she lived out her dream was alone worth the price of admission. That day was the fulfillment not just of one of her desires, but also of my desire to do another special thing for her. I do not think that day came about the way it turned out just because we lucked into finding, for example, that hotel room. Rather, it turned out as it did because it was what was supposed to be—just as her philosophy of life taught me to believe. Thanks, Mother, for the opportunity to have this memorable experience together with you in such a great place, around such a wonderful and special event. Not even the Super Bowl, World Series, or even the famous Rose Parade in Pasadena, California, could have been better than that day at the Rose Parade in Portland, Oregon.

There were special times and places for each child with Mother. There was the trip to the Holy Land in Israel that she always dreamed of, but never thought she'd see. It was orchestrated by sister Bertine, and sister Lorraine also went along to provide company. There was an unexpected trip to Japan orchestrated by sister Lucille and her husband. Mother marveled at another culture she knew little about except through her love of reading and a few collectibles. She brought back in her lap on the airplane a wonderful large, spun-glass lavender vase only our mother could have found made from an old soda bottle. That vase now occupies a special spot in our home. Then, there were all the wonderful times she enjoyed with brother Buzz, who remained and lived in Twin Falls. There were numerous theatre productions in Twin Falls in which Buzz had a major thespian lead. He and his family were the major link with Mother when all her children, except Buzz and Archie, moved from Twin Falls to pursue the dreams she had helped foster for each child. But, I suppose our sister Lucille set the standard of doing special for our mother as a shining act of thoughtful love and affection. Four simple words sum up that special event: Queen for a Day.

No, our mother was never Queen for a Day in the formal sense, although she was to achieve on her own a more outstanding award. For those who are much too young to know what Queen for a Day was, then a little background is in order.

Back in the late 40s and stretching over a twelve-year period, there was a very popular radio program known as "Queen for a Day." In today's television, you might think of it as a reality program that designates someone a royal Queen. You have to know or remember that this was the time just after the Second World War. Prices had been "rolled-back" to pre-war times and ceilings placed on them, and things had been in short supply during and immediately after the war. Mother often talked about the rationing of food, how hard it was to get this or that, and how you just had to learn to do without certain things. And so a radio program based on being Queen for a Day was a natural hit with its post-war audience. Being on the radio, compared to television today, a program on Queen for a Day conjured-up one's imagination even more for an audience who could not see who was being designated a Queen.

"Queen for a Day" proclaimed a dream day on which you received whatever your heart desired. In fact, what you got was a very nice package of sponsor's gift items. It was a bit like today's extreme makeover TV programs. The highly popular radio version of the program, that later moved to the just emerging television, worked as follows:

First, an audience, nearly all women, was gathered in a studio. Each woman was asked to write a brief account of something they really wanted which would make a dream of theirs come true. Based on what the show organizers were looking for, three contestants were selected and invited on stage to tell their story to a listening audience on radio across America. Those in the live audience rooted for their favorite contestant and got to vote by applause as recorded on a VU Meter. The highest level of applause determined who was selected as Queen for a Day. The winner was designated with a crown and title; thus, "Queen for a Day." It worked like a charm as far as radio programs went in those days coming after the Second World War, and the show was a big hit.

The radio version—there was a later television version—of the program usually originated and was broadcast out of Los Angeles. However, on occasion, the program would travel out to various small towns throughout the United States. Well, one day in came to—of all places—Twin Falls, Idaho.

Our sister Lucille, then 18 years of age, decided to be part of the audience. The program was being held in the Orpheum movie theater, one of three movie theaters we had in our small town. She had no intention of being one of the three contestants, but along with all the other women in attendance, she filled out a paper asking why she should be selected and what she would like if she were Queen for a Day. Having been one of the last to enter the theatre on that day, she was seated far up in the balcony on the very back row. Sure enough, when the lucky names were called, she was selected as one of the three contestants for that week's Queen for a Day program. She scurried her way from the balcony, screaming in disbelief all the way to the stage at her good fortune.

Each contestant was given about five minutes to tell a heart-wrenching story of life, what they desired, and then a series two or three questions were asked by the host, Jack Bailey. As each story unfolded in real time, the audience cheered, sobbed, and did the usual things that audiences do in such shows. Lucille's story was that she wanted a washing machine for her mother, and she really did. She described some of the conditions about where and how Mother did the family wash. Jack Bailey was to say about his long running show years later that, "It's—the show—not what they want, it's why they want it that counts with us." And Lucille won! She was crowned Queen for a Day and draped in a sable-trimmed red velvet robe and a jeweled crown. Jack Bailey then gave her various prizes and extolled the usefulness of each. There was a toaster, various gift items from local stores, and of course roses and a throne. As each item was presented her, Lucille cried and screamed aloud as any good contested would. But, the most memorable, grand prize was an agitator-type washing machine for her mother. This final gift was awarded while "Pomp and Circumstance" played at the end of the show. This surreal event captured a simple, yet elegant act of love that our mother never forgot. I think it was one of those special acts by one of her children that was more dear than any of the many awards and acclamations she received from so many civic organizations. Whether these were the tangibles of a washing machine or in the intangibles of dusting the furniture, Mother knew and we knew that each gesture really meant something to her and to us. Thanks, Mother, for the gift of sharing from the heart!

Lesson 9:
Have Faith, but Don't Act So Holy

My mother was the most religious and faith-based person I've ever known. You could catch her frequently praying in the most personal and silent way. It was as if she and God were having a personal and intimate conversation. Her head would be slightly bowed and moving ever so gently in a smooth up and down motion as if blown by a gentle breeze. Her lips barely quivered and seem to repeat words as if she was saying a rosary, but she was not Catholic except in the small "c" sense. I think she and the Tibetan monks had a lot in common. Prayer was a private time and because of its subtle nature not an act to show off to others. But, this and other signs of her faith were there to be known if one observed closely.

Mother went to church on a regular basis, although I can remember when she got mad at her church for reasons that she didn't want to talk much about. I am sure it was not a question of religious doctrine, because she was quite clear on her faith-based beliefs. Rather, she had been the chief organizer of the annual food booth at the county fair and I think someone complained, as can happen in volunteer organizations, that they were not getting their way about some issue and criticized her leadership. If there was anything that irked Mother, it was someone going behind your back on some issue and not having enough backbone to confront things head on, in her words, in "a working to solution" manner. She could take any criticism or suggestion, as long as you worked within the system— her local church in this case—with others to make things better. If you just wanted to complain or gossip about something, then do it in your own closet to yourself! She was clear on being up front in all her dealings—personal, business, political, or religious.

She liked reading the scriptures, but never used the scriptures as a defense of her position and actions. She knew many verses, but wouldn't quote them. You would witness first hand her love of the scriptures in the evening as she was lying down to sleep. On the night stand was a worn Bible. She would take it out, read a few passages or a chapter, and then lay it down before going to sleep. She didn't do that every night, but you could count on it at least a couple times a week. I suspect the other times she was just too "tuckered out," as she would say, from a long day's work.

I think that for her the Bible was a source into which one should enter to seek wisdom on how to live out love for self and towards others in community. On occasion, she would talk about some wisdom she had gained during her reading, and I am sure it served as a thread to action in her life. To me that was a tremendous lesson because it matched scripture—to living out what you learn in real life experiences, and not to rely on narrow passages to justify your position in judging others actions. You were not better because you read the scripture or could quote from it, but because you lived it by its overall message of community and love for others. She said that "God watches over you. We don't always get what we ask for, nor should we. God gives us what is necessary." Her grandmother had taken her to church, and I think she saw in her grandmother the tender love that she believed God provided as a result. All was really well if you just allowed your life to be lived through your faith. She gave herself over and was rewarded.

I think that is about as much as she would have liked me to write on the topic of religion and faith, so we will make this a short chapter, except to comment on the value of prayer as she so eloquently expressed on more than one occasion.

Prayer made a great deal of sense to my mother. She used it often in her own silent way as a means of thanks, rather than of asking for something. She once asked God, for example, "To let her live until her last child, then 7, became 15. I don't know why I hit on that age (of 15)," she laughed to a reporter who asked her. "I guess I thought he could support himself then if he had to." Sounds a bit like her own experience of life that changed for her at age 16! As the years went by, she changed her prayer for the strength to "Put her kids though college." Her prayer was answered. It's all pretty simple if you really think of it in the terms she did!

I already described what Mother said about why I was given the legal name, Danny G. Langdon. Of course Danny is a nickname and the G doesn't stand for anything. Her answer was, "That's the way it was meant to be!" That was her philosophy on lots of things. It was as if to say God or nature had ordained whatever it was to be, so you might as well get used to it. Stop trying to read any more into it or it will drive you crazy.

There was an instance between my junior and senior years of college. I worked during the summer as a television cameraman at the local TV station, where my brother was the Assistant General

Manager. I really liked the job because I got to do new and cool things. In those days the commercials were mostly "live," with people and products in front of the camera rather than on videotape. Of course it meant that all kinds of things could go wrong and did, but mostly it went well. There was our own local version of American Bandstand where the local kids came and danced, and I kind of felt like a big shot behind the camera. I remember going home a couple of weeks before college was about to start again towards my senior year and telling my mother how I might like to take a year off and continue with the camerawork before finishing my last year. I could see that look on her face as she listened carefully and reinforced the fact that I had enjoyed the work, but I could sense that she really thought it best that I go ahead and finish my last year. It wasn't so much the words she used, as it was the way she put it. "You know, it's meant to be that you should finish college first, and then you can decide if you really want to work in TV or not." I got the message. It was the right move. In fact, I decided that being a cameraman, for all its fun, wasn't what I wanted to be, and no extra year was going to make any difference. In fact, I went on to graduate school to get my master's degree in school administration and never regretted once that decision or her support for my advanced education.

By way of a summary, there is a connecting thread in the all the lessons described here. That simple message in the last story I just told: "That's the way things were meant to be!" I don't mean this in a spiritual way, which also may be true, but more in the certainty of having been instilled with confidence that no matter what I did, the results would be a lesson or experience of personal growth if I but allowed it to be. Or, it was an experience that would serve us well if we followed, not our mother's dreams, but what she helped us see the potential for. Mother was grateful for all the good and all the bad things that taught a lesson of what to do in the future. She trusted the hard times, believing that things would work out for the best. "Don't sweat the little things, find what works and build on it," she would say on many occasions. Don't let someone else beat down your dreams. As my good, personal friend, the late Gene J. Myers, once said to me, "Be the person who has always been inside you!" Thanks Gene, you must have known or been raised by a parent like our mother.

As Life Went on and Came to Its Inevitable and Accepting End

From the time our father died to her own passing at the age of 85, our mother never once flinched at life—squarely facing it for herself and for her family. It was a study in steadfastness, knowing that one simply had to be master of whatever life put in front of you. Have faith and do something about the challenges rather than complain or feel sorry for yourself. All will work out if you put your mind and action into facing life's opportunities and challenges.

Of course, facing life takes more than faith. It takes hard work and her kind of tough work as a scrap metal dealer was the benchmark against which anything else was a minor challenge by comparison. She took such delight in her work that it didn't seem hard for her to face anything else. She would, in fact, speak at times of how much harder others had it than she did. It is an example of that idiom, "Is the glass half full or half empty?" It is her own recognition that things could have been much worse, and indeed she had experienced some of that in growing up and learned from it. By her example, she expected no less from her children in whatever struggles we were surely to face throughout childhood and as adults. In simple terms, you were to face up to things, and not shrink under what is merely a burden. No surrender; move on!

After our father died, she indeed got up the next morning and went to work, and for 40 years thereafter. She generally worked six days a week, including most Saturdays. She considered Sunday a day of rest and other than some occasional social work for others, she would observe a day of rest. I don't think it was a religious thing with her, although there was a tinge of that maybe. Her practical side said, "Don't be nuts; you need the rest!"

Mother's Montage

Mother did not take many planned vacations. She did talk about the trip in 1937 to the Carlsbad Caverns and other parks that she and dad visited. They took Archie and Dorothy on the trip to Carlsbad Caverns. Later, when there were more of us kids, there was another vacation when we all went to Yellowstone Park that corners the states of Idaho, Montana, and Wyoming. Aunt Bessie, along with our dog Suzy, rode in the front seat of Mother's pickup, while we five kids rode all the way in the bed of the pickup under the brown canvas cover with a large, zippered rear opening. It was a fun trip, and I can still recall walking right up to and looking inside the Old Faithful geyser, as it was possible to do then, unlike today. But those few excursions were about the extent of true vacationing outside the immediate area of Idaho. We often made our way as a family to several nearby hot springs. We enjoyed skinny-dipping in the hot pools and would have a picnic with all the fixings. There were also the many times we went camping for the summer on the Little Wood River. My sisters fondly recall excursions with their mother to many community concerts and musicals. There was in particular the excursion to Salt Lake City on a business trip where they heard Harry Belafonte sing, and saw Don Beddoe, the well known character actor of the 30s and 40s, in concert. Our mother was a very literate and, in her own way, a very sophisticated lady, who sought to pass on to her children an appreciation for things of culture. That might seem paradoxical for a family living almost literally within a junk yard and a mother who was master with a cutting torch. But as she taught us to note about others, outward signs don't necessarily reflect inward driving forces, knowledge, and experiences. Today our husbands, wives, and children know that we learned such appreciation for things not entirely on our own, but by example from our mother.

Mother knew a great deal about the world. She could tell you facts about history and parts of the world she had never seen, but had only read about. She loved travel magazines, studied the pictures and write-ups in *LIFE* magazine, and wondered at the beauty of gardening in *Sunset* magazine. Late in life she loved the travel programs and TV's History and Discovery channels. Other than her long journey by train across America to come to Idaho, she had mostly traveled only around Idaho and some into Utah, Nevada, and California. Late in life she traveled with some of her children overseas, and when I was in the Peace Corps she came to Ethiopia where I was stationed as a teacher. In Africa she was overwhelmed by the rawness of the ordinary villager's life, yet the beauty and gentleness of the Ethiopian people whom she met and loved. I think she was particularly struck by the simplicity of life and what it took for people to merely survive, while all along with a smile on their faces as they worked and lived in community with one another. She knew instinctively by her own experience what these villagers were going through in terms of surviving day to day. She had experienced that! For a person who had not traveled extensively in the world, she knew the world pretty well.

I've attempted to describe several lessons learned both from the business side and numerous social outreaches of our mother's life, but there are a few other worthy experiences and observations to fully capture this special person.

While it was her husband who started the business, it was her own skill and tenacity that made it successful. She would typically arise at 6:00 to 6:30 a.m. and go off to work by about 7:00 a.m. That was, of course, unless someone had arranged with her to meet earlier because they had a load of scrap metal that had to be unloaded before they went off to early morning farming, or some other kind of work.

She generally had a group of three to five men working for her. The number depended on what was going on in the business at the time. If they were getting ready to load a railroad car or two with iron for shipment, then an extra two or three hands would be needed. These men were generally recruited through the local unemployment office, although there were some routine hands that she knew who always needed the extra money and had previously proven that they had the stamina to do the work. She would be loyal to anyone who showed the capacity to do the rough work and would rehire them without question.

Mother usually had two men on permanent hire. Each was a character study and worthy of some description because her hiring each tells something about her as a person and an employer. Undoubtedly, the most colorful character was a man by the name of Coy Prescott. Coy worked for and with Mother for a good 25 years. He became almost a part of the family and is still spoken of in terms of his odd nature, but also for his loving capacity to be nice to us kids. We knew very little about Coy's younger years, but that he was a veteran of the Second World War. I am confident that the war had some deleterious effect on him that went unmentioned and untreated, other than as indicated by occasional visits to the veteran's hospital. Coy had a brother who worked briefly for Mother, and a sister who lived in town. He was on the surface an illiterate man, void of social skills, unkempt, and almost scary to the unknowing. But he was always the one who wanted to know what I was doing, where I was going, and what I liked to do. He never forgot our birthdays and marked the occasions with simple presents, perhaps a comic book or some sweets. He was always there, even if Mother was off doing business elsewhere. He could be trusted to keep the business going, even when he could not answer sometimes a specific question from a customer or could not handle the counting of money very well. "You'll have to ask Marian that," or "Go see Marian to get paid," he would often say. He always referred to our mother by her first name, as if he knew her as a best friend, rather than as his employer. In a sense he did, but he was always at some respectful distance.

Coy loved reading comic books. He had stacks and stacks of them in his modest room in a local boardinghouse. We suspected he didn't know how to read and comics provided him a form of visual entertainment and delight that not knowing written words closed him out of. As life rolled by, he often passed on to mother's grandchildren his favorite comics. While he was the very same age as our mother, he looked as if he was forever sixty-years or more with his scruffy beard, usually unkempt attire, and few words that showed any real command of the English language. You knew he liked to drink, but had to avoid it as much as he could lest it run his life for him. His really bad habit was chewing tobacco. He had a "pinch of it," as those who use it refer to a wad of the disgusting stuff between their cheek and gums, in his mouth constantly. Worst of all, it meant spitting the juice that would be formed as the tobacco interacted with one's saliva onto the ground right in front or to the side of you as you were in conversation. Add to all these rather disgusting things the fact that he was never exactly clean. You might wonder how you could ever possibly stand to be around such an individual, let alone come to love him. As kids and adults we all spoke of Coy as the strange person he was, but always with loving affection. I think he was a great lesson in how to treat a person who can't help themselves. He was our Coy, and we loved him for what he was on the inside more than how he looked on the outside. When he died he was buried in one of the many burial plots that Mother owned. We all felt as if one of the family had left us. Indeed, it was so!

One other of our mother's work hands and also one of our favorite was an individual known to us as "Big Ernie." Ernie was a black man, very tall and stout. He lived just a little way down our street and over one block on 5th Avenue West. He worked for Mother for at least ten years.

Big Ernie was a gentle soul, very strong, and always kind to us children. He had brawny shoulders and the sweat ran from his arms and forehead as he shook hides to get the salt off. He could roll and pack a hide that normally required two men and easily toss it himself up and onto the awaiting flat bed truck. He stayed vigilant about his work, and given the physical demands it called for he should have faltered by the end of the day, but he never did. Mother credits him for much of the success that surrounded her business in that warehouse, and Ernie was a model to us not just as a black man, but as a real model of manliness and kindness. Certainly, he and Coy were men cut of different cloth, background, intelligence, experience and many things that make up a person, but they were both godsends to the success of our mother's business and to her children.

Of course, there were many, many other kinds of people who came in and out of her business as she hired this one and that one. Many were drifters passing aimlessly through our town.

Undoubtedly some had criminal records, but they never said anything, nor displayed any anti-social behavior. Although hardened on their exterior, some could not physically last an hour, let alone a day. I watched many a burly man wither under the demands of "packing" hides. They simply could not expend the energy and sweat it demanded, did not have the persistence needed to get the job done, or could not withstand work conditions in extreme heat or cold, constant flies, or the stench of horse or cow hide flesh. Some would simply walk off the job and some would not even walk in the side door to the warehouse once they saw the task at hand. Or they would stay once, but not return the second promised day. Maybe it was because of the work or their wandering travel that made up their life as a drifter, hobo, or drunk. Other men stayed and met the challenge because they had families to feed. Perhaps some stayed so as to not be outdone by the woman who worked beside them. Mother was always there, doing the hardest work on earth, and so were Coy and Ernie. It was the work at hand that had to be done. Many could appreciate it, but few could do it. It was one of the reasons that I was convinced that my mother could beat up anyone's father.

In the mid-1950s, due to advancements in textiles and synthetics, the market for fur, hides, pelts and wool became depressed and gradually faded. Mother moved out of those animal-based commodities and quickly changed the business to other market possibilities. That is why the scrap iron part of the business expanded in response to the Second World War and subsequent industrial growth that followed it. In today's terms, she was responding to worldwide market needs as any shrewd business person would have. For example, she later recognized the need for what is known as blacksmith iron. This kind of iron includes an array of iron rods, bars, sheet metal, and angle iron used to construct a variety of products for use in farming, manufacturing, and various kinds of processing. She began to deal in both new blacksmith iron, as well as recycling used iron as blacksmith iron at a cheaper price to meet the same needs. It was common for someone to come in and say that he needed a piece of six foot by two inch angle iron so that he could weld it to an implement he was making to process potatoes or fix some item for farming. He would specify his need and she would quote him a new- and a used-iron price. They might haggle a little, but each party knew the general price range and quickly came to an agreement. Then she would find a piece fitting the dimensions in the rack of new blacksmith iron or together they would look in various locations in the yard until they found the piece from an old plow handle, iron wheel support, boiler frame, thrasher, or other implement that could be torched from its original form to the new form. I would watch— or sometimes helped— her move the two tanks of gas and acetylene that were needed to fire the cutting torch. The tanks were mounted and held by chains to a two-wheel hand cart that could be led along paths between stacks of iron to the location where the cutting was accomplished. From the two tanks to the cutting torch there was a 25-foot length of rubber tubing through which the pure oxygen and acetylene would flow when valves and regulator meters were turned on the top of each tank. Often was the time I helped straighten-out the two hoses as they became tangled under a piece of iron sticking out from a pile of iron.

The cutting torch itself was a two-foot-long, narrow double tube-like device with a tip on the end that bent to a ninety-degree angle. She would hold the cutting torch firmly, and turn on the gases with small valves on the other end of the torch shaft. First was the acetylene gas. As the acetylene gas emerged from the tip of the torch, she lit the gas by making a spark from a "striker," and as this lit the gas and created a flame, she carefully turned on more of the oxygen supply with another valve. From the tip of the torch a bright, bluish/yellow flame burst forth which could be adjusted with just the right flow of oxygen and acetylene to be hot enough to cut iron. She would reverently bow her head a couple of times in what I always assumed was prayer, but was perhaps only thanks, and she would put the torch to the metal and begin cutting a swath through it. Before the metal was finally cut through and fell to the ground, it changed to a molten form as it dripped precariously to the ground and formed a neat pile of grayish-blue droplets. Small sparks of yellow metal flew in every direction during the cutting. Without goggles to wear over her eyes, she would have been blinded. Throughout the process you had to watch or feel for the sparks, lest they land on your skin or start a fire on your clothing or a nearby flammable object, such as oil or gas that had dripped from a punctured container or farm implement in the immediate area. Sometimes she recalls almost blowing up a gas tank that, unknown to her, still had some gasoline in an old junked car she was demolishing. She said more than once she hated demolishing old cars the most and in later years refused to buy them for fear of what disaster they might bring. Besides, there was little return to be realized for the excessive time it took to cut the junk cars into its various pieces.

To avoid the sparks of the cutting torch, she wore long-sleeved, usually plaid or light brown shirts, Levi pants, sometimes a canvas bib, and always cowboy boots which she found more comfortable. It was not unusual to see where a fire had started on her pant's leg and moved a ways before she discovered it and put it out with some nearby can of water. She was burned many times, but never seriously enough to miss a day's work. It was more common to see the results of hot sparks, not on her clothing so much, but those that had landed on and pock-marked her teeth. Fortunately, I suppose for her, she had long ago lost all her teeth to the neglect caused by lack of access to affordable dentistry in her early years. Thus, while she wore false teeth, she had one pair for work and another for other occasions. If you hadn't seen her put her teeth in or out or saw them soaking in a jar to clean them, you would have never known she wore false teeth. She never made a great deal of the fact that she wore false teeth and we never gave it a second thought ourselves. It is perhaps this description of her daily work and work attire that led more than anything to penning the title to this book, "My Mother Can Beat Up Your Father." Today in my office I have two of the strikers used by Mother to light the cutting torch she used in business. They are reminders of the hardship she endured, her strength of character, and the work she truly loved and so gladly did each day for her family to survive.

The physical cutting of iron was an initial, necessary first step that eventually culminated in preparing a shipment that would be sent to the mills as part of the process for making steel. The steel mills needed the iron in small pieces not exceeding a certain length, so that the iron could be placed in huge vats for smelting—heating— to make steel. In addition, the iron had to be somewhat free of dirt, excess oil, and other contaminates that might damage the vats, generate unwanted fires or heat, or mix with in the final step of making steel products. There was more to this processing of scrap iron as a commodity than met the naked eye.

Once the iron was cut to appropriate size and stacked in piles, there would come a time, about every two months, when a "shipment" was prepared for transport by rail car to the mills. The mills were the Geneva Steel Company or Utah-Pacific Pipe Company in Utah or the Luria Brothers' mill in Pueblo, Colorado. A shipment was composed of tons of cut scrap iron loaded into a long open-top railroad car with 8-foot sides. When fully loaded the car could be seen rolling through the farm land with spikes of protruding metal from the top of the car like needles on an angered porcupine's back. To get the cut iron to a railroad car for shipment was a major feat in and of itself requiring incredible physical strength and stamina. Our mother directed and participated as a co-worker in this process which was equal to the arduous task of cutting the iron.

As with "packing" of hides, she would hire a crew of two or three men to work along side Ernie and herself. Due to physical limitations, Coy never participated in this particular work, but was there to take care of the ever-present customer who had accumulated mountains of cut scrap iron in her various locations in town. The assembled crew would drive her International truck, with five foot iron sides, up to an iron pile, and using the combination of a hoist and physical labor, pick up the iron and place it in the back of the truck until it was full. She didn't have, as they do today, large magnets that make this loading much easier to do by the labor of a single person. It was mostly physical labor. However, one year she made a large, iron bucket contraption which held perhaps half a ton of metal that could then be hoisted using a crane mounted on a truck frame, and then dumped into the truck used to transport the iron. When the transportation truck was full, it was driven a mile or two to the railroading siding just past the Depot Grill where it had to be unloaded by hand and placed in the waiting railroad car.

At the railroad siding in Twin Falls there was a large wooden platform with a ramp at one end. You could drive the truck up and onto the platform. In that way, the pile of iron in the truck would be at eye level or just above the top of the rail car. The crew had to get into the bed of the truck and physically lift each piece of iron and throw it into the rail car. Imagine the physical strength and repetitive action it took to unload iron and fill the railway car. This meant thirty to forty trips back and forth from the iron piles to the rail siding. It took two to three days to complete the task and all along she was estimating, from her long experience, how many tons had been loaded as the mills would order a certain tonnage and you had to be pretty accurate not to exceed or be short on your load. If you were overloaded, the mill might pay less for the extra ton or two. If you were short, they would let you know about that in negative terms.

After she estimated what she felt to be a full and correct load of iron, she then had the rail car moved by a train engine to a point where a railroad agent would weigh the loaded car. She and the railroad agent would play this game of how close she was in her estimate and he would remark at her prowess and ability to be pretty much on the mark. He would hand her a printed copy of the weight slip, or bill-of-lading as they referred to it, and she paid the appropriate fee. Only then did she know for sure that x-tons of iron metal were being shipped as requested. If she was a little short of her estimate, she would take her pickup down to the yard and get a little more scrap to throw on top of the rail car. Better to be on target of what they requested than a little short, even if you didn't get paid for the little extra. Going along to help in some small way in the back of the pickup was a treat.

In so many ways, seeing the bustle of activity at the rail siding was fascinating. You could image how that load of iron joined other box cars and tankers on its journey with a hundred or more cars through the valleys and mountain before reaching its final journey at the mill. There at the mill the process of unloading was repeated by the mill through more advanced and less labor intensive mechanical and magnetic means. Mother's work was part of the vast chain of events that supported American industry and in her time made contributions to more than one war effort. The tanks, ships, farm, and industrial machinery, and the other implements of industry, scattered across our nation and other continents all utilized iron in one shape or another or products of steel made from iron. It seemed a bit of irony to her that what she helped create on one hand as new metal, might very well return again as scrap metal. Though she would never know for sure, some of that scrap might well have cycled its way through one of her yards perhaps two or three times over the forty years she was involved in this scrap to business to scrap again cycle. One day as we were standing in one of her lots, she pointed next door at a stack of new metal pipe that were to be used by the city for replacing some water mains in town. How ironic she said aloud that these very pipes were perhaps made from the scrap that had once lain in piles on one of her lots—perhaps right where we were standing that day. One can't help but wonder to this day where the fruits of her labor are scattered throughout the world.

Mother constantly kept an eye on the market conditions that surrounded her business—those market prices for every commodity she brokered. You don't just collect a bunch of scrap iron and ship it off any time you felt like it to the market place. Like any commodity—corn, wheat, oil or whatever—one must be aware of the prevailing market conditions in order to eventually get the best price for your commodity. This would include for her things like the price being paid currently or as a future per ton in the classic market sense of supply and demand. Sometimes the mills had enough scrap iron on hand and the price would be set low. Other times there was a shortage because of rising needs for steel for cars and other manufacturing and the price per ton would be higher. You hoped that price for scrap iron would be up and you had paid a lower price and accounted for your amount of labor, wages, oxygen and acetylene fuel for the cutting torch, gasoline and maintenance for trucks, and on and on. Then, you had to control how much scrap you would buy, what price to pay, and where you would pay rent to store it, and how that all this would affect overall costs. She knew all these things in her head and kept her eye on when it was best to be ready to sell to the mills. Sometimes her timing was right on and she got a good price, had plenty of supply and labor costs were modest. Other times, she had no choice and received little for her labor and times could be tough for a while. She always said, however, that "Things would get better!" She would be prepared for those better times and as an independent entrepreneur she was astute in these matters of commerce. Frankly, I am inclined to believe that Allan Greenspan, the leading economic guru of our century really had little over the fundamental good common sense that our mother had about how the economy functions; albeit on a small scale, but fundamentals are fundamentals. Besides, she did her own accounting books around a system she devised herself, and I can assure you that those books were immaculate, complete, and could withstand any audit they might have faced. I can further report that she and the Internal Revenue Service were on good terms, although I am pretty sure they were not in a position to know much about the scrap metal business.

Our mother knew all along that there was a time and an opportunity to be in the kind of business she was in. It had its heyday during the Second World War and for roughly 25 years or so thereafter, as domestic and international business grew. Scrap iron in particular would be an okay business to remain in, but just as the business in hides and pelts would fade, so would the scrap metal business change with competition from cheaper foreign markets. As a small-time player, she gradually would be a victim of a global economy. Although she didn't say so directly, I think that in part that is why she did not encourage us to take over the business one day, even though my brother Buzz had indicated some interest in doing so. I think she believed each one of us should pursue that which our talents and hearts would lead us to. It was a lesson learned without having to say so.

She continued in the business herself until such time she no longer had the physical strength to pursue such a demanding job and business. At the age of 75 she formally retired. She slowly sold off the remaining scrap over a five-year period until the business was only a memory. She once said of her scrap metal business, "I wouldn't trade it for any business in the world—I really enjoy it! The people I meet and the things I buy make my business interesting to me." She went on to conclude, "I have to laugh at some people who wonder why a woman runs this type of business. Well, I can say one thing, it sure beats sitting behind a desk. A couple of days of that and I'd be so mean I couldn't get along with anyone."

While she maintained a successful business for nearly 40 years on her own, I am sure you have noted that she was the epitome of a person concerned with social peace and justice. I could never totally figure out what the driving force was for her to help so many in need and to serve in so many volunteer organizations. I know it wasn't to be known and recognized for her work by others. She never sought, or expected recognition. It naturally came and she was humble and unassuming. I believe that she did all this because it brought a true joy and sense of accomplishment to her, while contributing in ways that she knew others appreciated. She could be equally a member or the leader of a group, but especially a leader because she knew how to organize, inspire and get others to do what was needed. If not, she would gladly do it herself.

Among women she was admired. Among men she was perhaps a puzzle because she did what they did and often better. It was quite common, for example, for men of leadership in the steel mills, hide industry and others she dealt with to send her holiday gifts. While they typically exchanged bottles of liquor among themselves, they made sure to send her huge boxes of chocolates, accompanied with nice pens and notes of appreciation for her business savvy. Later in life, many of these boxes of chocolates found their way to her children with families of their own. Those grandchildren deeply appreciated the wonderful flavors—much as she had herself from her Aunt Bessie's chocolate boxes while growing up.

Her time in history was when women were supposed to be in the home and in aprons, but she was also in the world of work as an equal made of her own efforts. Remember, these were the times of the 1940s, 50s, 60s, 70s, and 80s. It's odd that she didn't support in later years an organization like NOW (National Organization of Women) for she represented what they wanted for women. She could have been their president and the symbol of a successful woman. Don't misunderstand, she didn't think NOW as an organization wasn't needed. Rather, I think she truly believed that women were capable of getting what they should by standing up and getting it on their own, organized or not. Perhaps her very model of a working woman demonstrates that self-confidence is in the eye, heart and actions of the beholder. Believing in something is easy. Believing and achieving that end means not letting anyone or any circumstance keep you from doing or achieving it. I, for one, surely learned confidence as a lesson of life that I practice in pursuing my own dreams. As a business model-maker trying to define the role of humans at work, consultant and author of work understanding in business today I find that confidence takes me a long way. I learned from her a great deal about what work was, but more so I learned how to have the self-confidence and tenacity to pursue success despite what others sometimes thought of my dreams.

When it came finally time to "retire," I am not sure she exactly knew what the word meant. Of course, for physical reasons brought on by age she had to leave the scrap metal business behind her. She had no nest egg, so it was natural and logical for her children to purchase a home and move it and her to live on our sister Bertine's farm. "It was a good move," as she put it, and she never looked back. She had not saved a dime to my knowledge, but retirement money would not be needed. She never asked, but we knew what was needed and led by our sister on the farm we provided whatever financial support was required to make her life comfortable, and if more was needed it was provided. It wasn't a requirement on our part, but an act of love for someone who had given all of herself and so much more to us. So much for that! It should be some kind of law, if not moral code, that we be required as humans to provide for those who cared for us. If they didn't care of us in that loving way, that may seem like another matter, but probably not. I know in our case, it was not a question that needed any pondering. It was a foregone conclusion that came from pure love.

Even in retirement she continued to be socially active with things to do for others. She once said of retirement, "I feel sorry for people who have nothing to do but watch TV and think of their aches and pains." She had no sooner moved to the farm, taken a well-deserved breath—it probably lasted about that much time—than she started a new chapter of her life that lasted ten more years. In her view, a rocking chair was a thing of beauty to look at, not sit in.

Her new home was a double-wide, four-bedroom, what they call a prefabricated home that was quite attractive and that she adored. She reserved one room for her bedroom, of course, but also set up an office area to spread out her continued business interests in antiques and other collectibles. That left two entire bedrooms for an assortment of collectibles, as well as every spare inch of the living room, dining room, and kitchen that she could fill with antiques. The house could hold only so much, but she had access to my sister's old milk barn on the property to store box after box of glass, pottery, hats, branding irons, odds and ends of paperwork, etc., etc. Of course, that wasn't enough, so Bertine opened up two garage units on the property and left the cars intended for such use outside.

Around the property that surrounded her home she planted her beloved roses bushes with poetic names like Peace, Queen Elizabeth, and scores of others. She simply loved roses, and I think in their varying beauty they reflected her own inward and outward beauty of character and physical presence. To these she added a complementary willow tree that she loved sitting under, and an assortment of flowers she attended to with loving care. There, organized among her flowers, was an assortment of her favorite collectibles from the scrap metal business—an old plow, a butter churn, an old wood stove, a blacksmith forge, old insulators, and the like. She continued to lift and lug around any heavy object as if aging into her eighties was merely a change in numbers, rather than body morphing from quite natural degeneration. She could easily pick up a 50-pound sack of salt needed for her water softener. Her grandson, Barry, tells of the time he and some friends were having difficulty unloading a heavy object from his friend's pickup. As they pondered what to do, Mother walked over and picked up the object with apparent ease. His friends were amazed, but Barry knew that that was his grandmother at her usual best.

After moving to Bertine's farm in New Plymouth, Mother joined the local Payette Methodist Church, Payette Lorraine Chapter of the Eastern Star, met with other members of the Priscilla social club, and volunteered regularly at the local senior center. She became an excited fan of her favorite sport, basketball, as she watched her grandchildren play at the local high school and cheered and felt their pain at any loss, and would encourage the play of the next game.

She delighted in helping her youngest grandchild, Charlie, with his FFA project of raising chickens and selling eggs. When he went off to college, she and my sister continued to raise and dress chickens for several years. She always had her meals with Bertine's family in their home a mere seventy feet from door to door. She attended college graduations, made trips back to Twin Falls to see old friends and attend funerals. Having the farm as her home allowed her the freedom she never had otherwise to do all the things she had wanted, indeed earned. Of her life there, she once remarked with so much insight that, "It's hard to realize that you can get to a place in life where when you start a new day the time in it is your very own." Of course, she filled those days, not in solitude as so many retired are prone to do, but with others and being of service to others. The day before her sudden death, she had chaired her local church's holiday bazaar. That was that so much like her!

In 1952, long before her retirement, our mother was selected Mother of the Year for the state of Idaho. She had been picked to represent Twin Falls County and to compete with other Idaho mothers from the various geographic areas of the state. Appropriately enough, she was sponsored by the Business and

Professional Women's club of which she had been a long time, founding member and for which she had once served as the President. Endorsements for her nomination came from several local service groups, including the Twentieth Century Club, the Soroptimist Club, Twin Falls Parent-Teacher Association council, the Chamber of Commerce, Young Women's Christian Association and the local Boy Scouts of America. The range of her sponsorships for this honor alone says volumes about how well she was known and respected in her community.

In May of that same year she competed with mothers representing every state in the union and was selected as the national runner-up to another mother from Maine. According to their charter, the Mother of the Year event, coinciding with national Mother's Day, celebrates the "character truly representative of the ideals of mothers everywhere." The following qualifying criteria of Mother of the Year are exemplary of her life:

- A successful mother as evidenced by the character of her children
- Reflect strong religious and spiritual integrity
- Embody the traits of courage, patience, affection, kindness, understanding
- Homemaking ability highly regarded in mothers
- In life and conduct exemplify the precepts of the golden rule
- Have a sense of civic and international understanding
- Been active in community betterment or service for the public
- Be qualified to represent mothers of America

Being selected Mother of the Year was an honor that touched her very soul and for which she was forever grateful. She was honored for many other things during her life time, including being recognized as Business Woman of the Year, but it was the Mother of the Year that touched her so. For her children, it was a badge of honor we knew she deserved. She holds the record, we believe, as the youngest mother ever selected as a Mother of the Year in the state of Idaho.

As part of her recognition as Mother of the Year, she traveled to New York City to attend the *National Mother of the Year Conference*. There she received a further honor as the national runner-up. It seemed a bit of an irony that she made this trip on the same rail line as when first she came to Idaho at the age of four with her grandmother from the state of New York. The trip back to New York must have brought forth many memories for her of that first trip in 1915.

She stayed at the famous Waldorf Astoria Hotel in New York City, which was a big deal in those days. She also traveled to Washington, D.C. to meet with the U.S. Congressmen and Senators of Idaho and to be recognized for her accomplishment. But it was the side trip she took while in New York to her birth place in Jamestown that was most poignant.

She had hoped to see the mother that she never had, or who had been perhaps taken away from her. She had not seen or talked to her mother in 37 years, nor could she remember her mother since she left when she was but four years old. But alas it was too late. Her mother had passed away a mere six months before. She did meet and make contact with her mother's second husband. That was some closure, but surely not enough. Fairytale endings don't always happen, and if it wasn't meant to be, she accepted the ending for what it was. She moved on and never regretted the meeting that was never to be.

Just before Christmas, 1996 our mother passed away peacefully while standing in the kitchen of my sister's home in New Plymouth, Idaho. As in life, in death she died with no lingering illness, no apparent concerns, and as active as ever. Her approach to death (and indeed she probably had one) was that death was merely a natural and acceptable part of living. She was secured and assured by her faith and the knowledge that she had first and foremost successfully raised her children, and then and only then had she been successful professionally and served others who needed and wanted her help.

At the moment of her death I was in Africa on a business trip that blended into a vacation to visit Ethiopia where I had served in the Peace Corps, and then on to other parts of East Africa to visit Kenya and what was once the country of Tanganyika (now Tanzania). When I received a telephone call from my sister Lucille of her passing, I was just entering the Serengeti plains of Tanzania on a safari to see the wild creatures of Africa. As I wandered, along with my wife, in a Land Rover among the thousands of wild animals, we bounced on dusty roads. It was the perfect time to reflect on my mother's life that was as vast as the open, grassy plains before me. The splendid beauty of nature was the perfect place to be. The time could be used to reflect, grieve, heal, and give thanks in wave after wave of emotion. I could feel her presence right there with me.

Of course I cried, but it was in the beauty of the surroundings more a time to rejoice for a life fully lived and many lessons learned. At one point, I remember especially, that I had my head bowed and was, as I recall, thinking about her and my life with her as a boy. That must have gone on for several minutes of reflection, when I suddenly looked up roused from my deep thoughts by a hard jolt of the vehicle on the rugged road. There before me was a sight that was breathtaking and spiritually uplifting. The Land Rover, with its open top, allowed me to immediately stand up and there for miles around me were thousands of wild animals. There were hundreds of wildebeests, giraffes, and gazelles of all sorts, hyenas, zebra, and other creatures great and small. The entire group was in migration across the vast African plain, and they weaved as if crossing highways in and over the plain, stretching as far as the eye could see. Nature was in its mighty glory as if saluting the many thoughts I was having of my mother. It gave me the time in a perfect setting to reflect on her life so that when we returned to America and to the valley she was to be buried in, we could celebrate her life more than mourn her passing. She was buried with an Indian wool blanket as she had requested. Her sunset was brilliant. Her smile, confidence, love, warmth, and humor present. She often remarked when reflecting on her children, "You kids!" in an expression of fond stories we told about life with her and we laughed together. Or she would simply say, "You Betcha!" to something that was so obvious to her about what life puts in front of each of us.

Thanks forever, Mom!

Tributes from
Her Grandchildren and Others

She was strong beyond a measure
That most could hope to be;
Filled with a rugged independence
And a spirit of resiliency.
She testified in word and deed
To a kindness and a grace
That was freely shared with others,
Like the smile upon her face.
She sent me rubber-coated baseballs
When I was thousands of miles away.
"Don't ever want you to go without"
Is what I heard her say.
There was a silver dollar buckle
And "spud bars" by the pound.
Then, whenever I would thank her,
I'd hear that familiar sound.
"You betcha, sweetie. You betcha, dear.
That's what grandma's are for."
Then another special time would come
And she would show her love once more.
Memories and photographs
Are priceless treasures for this time,
Providing rich reunions
For the gathered ones she's left behind.
Final words are never easy
And tell only a small part;
I'll miss you Grandma—You betcha,
But, I'll keep you in my heart.

 —By Mitchell Langdon Townley
 Grandson of Marian Langdon
 Written for her memorial service, December 28, 1996

How Did You Know?

When I was eight or nine or ten
You sent me a box of trinkets.
A box of baubles and of jewels
You picked up at your last conference.
I spend hours milling through that box
Of key chains and sorted measures
And carried it throughout the house
Like the sultan's royal treasures.
I think of it from time to time
How I loved those things back then.
How did you know just what to get
A girl of nine or ten?

> —Written by Kristen Townley Puckett
> Granddaughter of Marian Langdon
> For her memorial service
> December 28, 1996

Free Verse Offered by a Friend
Just Before Her Death:

She bought raw hides, salted them down
Until she sold them to the tannery.
Wearing bib overalls and irrigator boots,
She would wade out onto the pile of hides,
Scrape off excess blood and salt,
Fold each hide into a three-foot square,
Help throw them onto the truck,
Heavy hides, still leaking blood.
She bought sheep pelts, they stink worse.
She was a market for scrap metal and junk.
Her voice was rough and her talk was tough,
A widow with a business to run
And kids to raise.
On most Sundays they were in church,
Clean and attentive, she in a dress.

—Written by Mr. Leonard Fields in October, 1995
Sent to the pastor of the United Methodist Church, Payette, Idaho
on the occasion of Marian Langdon's funeral in 1996.

In his letter Mr. Field's stated, "I have fond memories of her from
long ago. In 1947, or a while, I was the trucker to whom she threw
those hides. Believe me, she was a very respected and honored
person."